SECOND E...

START YOUR OWN
SENIOR
CONCIERGE
SERVICE

From Startup to

Success in Just 30 Days

CRAIG WALLIN

Dedication

If you've been downsized, outsourced, grown tired of the rat race or just need more income and a brighter future, this book is for you. If you're ready to take charge and become your own boss, this book is for you.

Since I published the first edition of this guide, I've heard from many readers who have started their own profitable local senior concierge service. I'm thankful they have shared their stories, because their contributions have made this second edition a bigger, better and more useful guide. Thank you all!

Thanks for buying this guidebook and may your new senior concierge service thrive and prosper!

How To Use This Book

I'm proud of you! You're doing something that most of us only dream about but never begin - starting your own business. There are many steps that go into starting a business, and it can seem like an impossible task. Where do I start? What should I do first? Who can I turn to for help? Now, with this step-by- step guide you will have the help you need to start your own successful and profitable senior concierge business.

You should plan to follow the startup steps listed in the guide to get your new business well underway in about a month. If you think 30 days is not enough time, just remember Mark Zuckerberg wrote the first version of Facebook in just 30 days! So what are you waiting for? Let's get started.

Table of Contents

Introduction

10,000 baby boomers a day will turn 65 – every single day between now and the year 2030. Add that to almost 50 million seniors in America today, and you've got a lot of customers for a senior concierge service. By 2030, there will be over 70 million Americans over 65 – one out of every five Americans!

Those older folks will live longer and have more money to spend, thanks to an era of prosperity during their working years. As seniors age, they need more help with many of the daily activities that younger folks take for granted, such as running errands, pet care, grocery shopping, driving to appointments, household management, and dozens of other tasks.

To provide that assistance to this rapidly growing population of seniors requires a special person called a senior concierge. The term "concierge" comes from the French term *"Comte des Cierges"* or keepers of the keys. Traditionally, the concierge worked in a hotel or luxury apartment building, assisting the guests or tenants with their every request.

Today, concierges assist busy executives, couples with two incomes but no free time, individuals and seniors by doing what their clients are too busy or unable to do themselves.

A good concierge is a capable, resourceful problem solver who is happiest when helping their clients with whatever challenge comes their way. About 70% of the personal concierges in the U.S. and Canada are women, and 30% are men.

A senior concierge can also benefit the children of seniors, the "sandwich generation," who also have to work and raise their own children. With help from a senior concierge, visits to their parents can be more about quality time together rather than having so many responsibilities to deal with at every visit. This is much less stressful for both seniors and their adult children.

According to concierge industry insiders, personal concierge services have become a multi-billion-dollar industry, with steady growth and great prospects for the future, especially in a recession-proof niche like senior concierge services.

As boomers become seniors and move into their "golden years," their needs and abilities change. While they prefer to stay in their own homes as long as possible, they realize they simply can't do it all, due to mobility and health challenges. This creates a golden opportunity for those who can provide assistance to seniors in need.

A senior concierge service can keep you as busy as you wish, whether you live in a smaller community or a big city. It requires no formal education or expensive training, just common sense, organization, honesty, compassion for elders and above all, a can-do attitude.

A senior concierge service can be started with very little money – if you have a car and a cell phone, you're almost there. Business printing, such as business cards, advertising flyers and forms can be created very inexpensively at your local copy shop or from the online printers listed in the resource chapter.

You'll also find forms in the back of this book for your own use – ready to customize with your business name, address and phone number.

The rewards of being a senior concierge are great – not just in dollars and cents – but in helping seniors live better lives by helping them enjoy their independence as long as possible. That's priceless. Another reward is that you'll have a flexible schedule to allow you to balance your everyday family life with your client's needs and projects.

Rates

Rates for private senior concierge services range from $20 to $60 per hour nationally. Rates are higher in large cities and lower in smaller towns and rural areas where the cost of living is lower.

With rates of $20 to $60 per hour of billable time, you can see it's possible to earn a solid income of $40,000 to $120,000 per year, depending on the rates where you live, and how many hours you work.

Best of all, a senior concierge service is a recession-proof business. People grow old and require your help and services regardless of what the national economy is doing. In addition, there is no expensive training or college classes required, as you can earn while you learn.

Of course, you should not expect to earn the maximum when you're just getting started. Most concierge service providers report that it takes about a year to become well known and in demand in the community.

Are You Ready?

Before making the decision to start your own senior concierge business, it's wise to take a good look at your personal strengths and weaknesses to see if this business really makes sense for you. Consider asking your spouse or partner as well. Here are the questions you need to ask yourself:

- ✓ Are you a caring, compassionate person? Your clients will be senior citizens, some with health conditions, who require patience and understanding. Also, because many are home-bound, they may be socially isolated and need a friendly listener and a cheerful smile.

- ✓ Are you an energetic person? Whether you are a part-time senior concierge or full-time, running a business is hard work. You need to be ready to work occasional 12-hour days, work odd hours when necessary, and answer phone calls from clients, service vendors and prospects day or night.

✓ Are you motivated? You will need to stay motivated after the initial excitement of launching your new business wears off and the day-to-day grind sets in. Of course, knowing you're the boss now, and are earning an independent, growing income will help strengthen your motivation!

✓ Are you organized? Being able to manage your time well, and all the other aspects of your new business are critical to your success. You'll find tips and advice in the chapters that follow that help you to get – and stay – organized so you can get more done in less time with less stress.

✓ Are you a people person? A senior concierge is all about people, from clients to prospects and others, such as tradespeople, you'll manage from time to time. If you'd rather be playing video games than meeting a new person, you may want to consider another business. But if you can handle the occasional cranky client or vendor and keep smiling, you'll do well in this business.

✓ Are you a self-starter? When you start your own business, it's up to you to make things happen. There is no more boss to turn to – it's just you and another deadline or appointment. From scheduling to organizing, you're in charge, and the project won't get done until you dig in and do it! Again – the rewards are great – for example, when you land a new client or get a grateful note from a client's kids who love what you've done for their mother or dad.

CHAPTER ONE
Senior Concierge Services

When you develop your list of concierge services, take some time to think about your skills and your comfort zone. For example, if you don't have experience organizing a move for a senior, don't offer that as a service until you've assisted on two or three moves, or worked on one as an unpaid volunteer to gain experience.

Another approach is to be honest with your client, telling them: *"I've never done that before, but I'm willing to help and learn."* That's the "can-do" attitude common to all successful senior concierges. Think of a new project that may be unfamiliar to you as a challenge, not an insurmountable obstacle.

Another option is to find a capable service provider who has the experience to do the job well, such as a senior relocation specialist or a home repair handyman. You'll learn how to find the best ones in a later chapter. Here are the top twenty-two in-demand services, listed in alphabetical order provided by senior concierges today:

Bill-paying and correspondence. Many seniors realize their memory is not as good as it once was, and welcome help with routine bill paying and other routine correspondence. They may not be aware or able to use the online bill paying options provided by most banks, or deal with issues that occur often with bills from service providers like cable and water utilities, or the yard care service.

A sign that a senior may need help is bills that go unpaid or too many charity donations. Often seniors who respond to solicitations from charities to save the orphans, the endangered species or the homeless folks at the mission end up on a mailing list of donors that is sold to scammers and fraudulent charities. You can protect them and be their "personal watchdog."

By getting those bills paid on time and protecting your clients from fraud, you are making their lives less stressful and safer – perhaps even saving them money in the bargain! When possible, encourage your clients to stay involved as much as possible in the bill paying process so they feel they are still in control, but have been relieved of the burden of day-to-day responsibilities.

Computer & technology help. Even younger seniors can be baffled by the complexities of computers, software and the high-tech appliances and gadgets often found in today's homes. If you have the basic skills, and are not intimidated by technology, this can be a valuable service to provide. If not, you can help your clients locate folks with these skills.

As one client said in frustration, *"I just want it to work!"* Computer services you could offer are: Teaching your clients how to use their computer, updating software, virus scans, organizing and digitizing photos or music, managing the email inbox, adding software, doing a home inventory for the insurance company or heirs, and digitizing it, help with I-pads, tablets and smartphones.

Daily check-in. Seniors, and their adult children who live too far away to visit regularly, appreciate having someone call or visit regularly to make sure everything is okay, and if not, being there to help.

After each visit, you can call or email the relative who requested the visits to let them know that their parent is safe and secure. This simple, yet powerful service can bring so much peace of mind for those who are unable to visit regularly.

A safeguard visit lasts about a half-hour, and you follow a simple checklist that includes the following areas, plus any items that a relative may ask you to check:

- ✓ Personal safety check. Take a quick look around to see if there is anything that could cause a fall or other accident.
- ✓ Observe appearance and demeanor – any changes from the last visit?
- ✓ Monitor medications – make sure your client is taking their medications as required.
- ✓ Check room temperature and adjust thermostat if necessary.

✓ Companionship. Sit down with your client and talk about what's happened in their life since the last visit, and what they have planned for the coming days. Find out if there is anything you can do for them in addition to the regular safeguard visit.

Because this is a short visit, and you'll need to allow for commuting time to and from the client's home, the cost is higher than your normal hourly rate. For example, if you visit for a half-hour, spend ten minutes each way driving to their home, and five minutes emailing your findings to the client's relative, you'll have about an hour invested.

De-cluttering. Most seniors have lived in their home for a long time, and that can cause "stuff" to accumulate. When the closets, garage, attic or basement are full, it's time for de-cluttering. Doing so can make it easier to maintain the home and make it easier for seniors and their family to make a smooth transition to a smaller residence, such as a retirement home.

What to do with all the accumulated items? A proven method is to start 3 piles. The first is items to be given to family and friends, the second for donations to local charities, and the last for saleable items that are worth listing on craigslist.org or ebay.com.

If you're not able to handle the selling part for your client, there are individuals who specialize in listing and selling items on E-bay for a fee, usually about 30% of the final sale price. To find an "E-bay helper" to assist you, visit: www.sellforme.ebay.com

Another option, but one that may not bring in as much money, is a good old-fashioned garage sale.

Escort service. Seniors who no longer drive need an escort to get them to social events and church services, and to be a companion while there.

Grocery shopping. Not everybody likes to shop for groceries, so this is one of the most popular services for a senior concierge. Also, there are seniors who have no choice, such as homebound seniors, or those with health issues or a handicap, that prevents even a simple trip to the supermarket.

For all those seniors who are too busy or unable to get to the store or just dislike grocery shopping, hiring a personal grocery shopper can be the perfect solution, and one that more and more are choosing. Having someone do the grocery shopping can even save money for many clients, who lose control at the supermarket, buying products they don't really need or shouldn't eat. That's why the snack food aisle at the supermarket is so large!

Grocery Shopping Tips

Whether you choose to computerize your grocery shopping records or use a simple card system, the first step should be to create a customer information card for use when a customer calls. Here's a sample to copy:

Customer name: _____

Address: _____

_____

City, State, Zip code: _____

_____

Home phone: _____ Cell phone: _____

Services requested: _____

Price: _____

Extra services: _____

_____

Date of service: _____

Favorite grocery store: _____

Pharmacy: _____

Total cost: _____

Date paid: _____

Ask your grocery shopping customers to phone in or email their shopping list at least a day in advance so you can better organize your shopping stops. Many customers prefer the telephone instead of fax or email, and it gives you an opportunity to ask any questions you may have about brands, sizes, etc.

Pay for each customer's order separately. Many customers will want to go over their individual receipts when you drop off the groceries, and a combined bill will make that difficult.

You'll need to have someone at home when you arrive with the groceries. Either let your customers know when to expect you – 3 to 5 p.m., for example, or get a key for your regular customers who cannot always be at home. A key release form is included in chapter five.

Set up a file folder for each regular customer and put the customer service cards in each customer's folder after they are paid. Some business owners keep a file of customer grocery preferences as well, so they can make sure to get the right brand or size.

Keep several nesting plastic totes and coolers in your car or van so you can keep each customer's grocery order separate. Put the receipt for each customer's purchases with the items so it will be easy to find when you deliver each order.

Keep a felt tip pen handy so you can write the customer's name on each bag as the grocery store clerk is bagging the groceries. This will help prevent order mix-ups.

Always keep your cell phone handy and turned on so your customers can reach you with requests for last-minute items or emergency prescription pickups.

Check with your regular customers once a month and ask "How am I doing?" This regular feedback will help you address any specific issues and ensure that your customers remain happy and loyal to you. Don't forget to ask those happy customers for referrals, as that is the most credible form of advertising – and it's free!

You'll find forms you can use for your grocery shopping customers in chapter 5, including a grocery delivery order form and a key release form.

Holiday helping. For many seniors, the holiday season can be a depressing time, as they remember lost loved ones or are unable to be with family living hundreds of miles away. In many cases, seniors must also deal with the reality that they can't move around as they did in their younger days. This loss of mobility can make it difficult to decorate or shop for gifts. But you can help your senior clients beat the holiday blues.

During the holiday season, a senior concierge can provide companionship, assistance with visiting friends, decorating their home, shopping and help their clients write and send holiday cards to family and friends.

Another outside activity that's sure to lift a senior's spirits is a drive around town to view Christmas decorations. Be sure to

START YOUR OWN SENIOR CONCIERGE SERVICE

take the time to listen – really listen – to your senior clients. Sit down with your client and talk about what's happened in their life since the last visit, and what they have planned for the coming days and the New Year. Find out if there is anything you can do for them to make their holiday better. That conversation can boost their spirits and help them beat the holiday blues. Oh, and don't forget the eggnog!

Home care. Homes always need work, from the simple tasks like vacuuming and dusting to the complex ones, like replacing a toilet float valve or a water heater. Because it covers such a wide range of projects, and requires regular attention (washing windows, for example) bringing home care under your senior concierge umbrella can provide a steady stream of work and income for a capable concierge. And most of your clients will be relieved that they are free of that responsibility!

Depending on your schedule or your skills, you may want to tackle some of the routine projects yourself, such as routine maintenance. Specialized projects that require a contractor, such as plumbing, electrical or furnace maintenance, can be handled by an outside business.

When you act as a "home services organizer," one of the many hats worn by a resourceful concierge, you can locate and recommend outside service providers to do the required work and collect a referral fee from the contractor for the recommendation. This is covered in detail in a later chapter, including a form for your use.

It is not uncommon for a concierge to earn a supplemental income from referral fees of several hundred dollars every month. Major projects, like roofing or furnace replacement, can cost thousands of dollars, and 10% of each one can add up fast.

The best way to win your client's loyalty is to set up a maintenance schedule for the house, so that routine maintenance gets done as needed. You can use a simple logbook to track the work, such as an inexpensive day planner, or set up a schedule on a computer, using Google Calendar or other scheduling software.

Home checks. Every fall, millions of seniors migrate to a warmer sunny climate, and back again in the spring. They are called "snowbirds", and the empty houses they leave behind, in both cold and warmer climates, can mean more profits for you.

One of the best sources of steady, dependable, supplemental income for a senior concierge can come from your existing customers. You've helped them when they are at home, and you can also help them with their empty house while they are gone.

Instead of losing the weekly income from helping them, you can replace it with another equally valuable service and provide peace of mind for them. Best of all, they know and trust you, so it's not difficult to persuade them to trust you with the care of their home while they are away.

If you live in the snowbelt, you can provide home check services for your customers who have gone South for the winter. If you're in the sunbelt, you can do the same when they head North in the spring.

If they need convincing, tell them about the retirees who left their Tampa home to spend the summer in the cooler Northwest. No one was checking their home, so when the air conditioner lost its refrigerant charge, it continues to blow hot, moist air around the home.

That encouraged mold growth, and when they did return, everything, including the furniture, was covered in a fine coating of white mold. The repair bill, which the insurance company did not cover, was over $20,000.

These home checks are usually done weekly, for a flat fee ($36 is a typical charge). Here is a list of the most common checks included in a "safe & secure" home check:

- Check exterior and interior for plumbing leaks and insect or rodent damage.
- Dispose of newspapers and door hangars.
- Flush toilets and run faucets.
- Check light bulbs on timers.
- Security check on all doors and windows.
- Check security system, if needed.
- Water plants if needed.
- Send "all okay" email to customer!

A good book about providing home watch services is: **Start Your Own Home Watch Business**, available at Amazon.com

Home organizing. Helping clients get organized is a common task for a senior concierge. A good home organizer can turn chaos and clutter into a functional, usable space, from the smallest closet or file cabinet to the largest garage or attic.

The most common areas in need of re-organizing are attics, bathrooms, closets, garages, home offices and kitchens. A serious do-over may involve new cabinets, closet systems, and remodeling tasks such as painting. If the project requires outside contractors, you can stay involved, and get paid for your time, as a project supervisor, screening and managing the workers involved and vendor commissions.

If you love organizing spaces for your senior clients, you may want to offer your services to other seniors in town. There will always be a steady demand for this service, and it's an excellent way to get acquainted with new prospects for your concierge services.

One proven approach is to offer a "one-day makeover" to new clients. Your client picks the most needy area of their home, and you go to work!

To improve your skills and knowledge of home organizing, I suggest you read these excellent books on the topic:

- ✓ *"Organizing from The Inside Out – The Foolproof System For Organizing Your Home and Office."* By Julie Morgenstern

- ✓ *"The Life-Changing Magic of Tidying Up – The Japanese Art of Decluttering & Organizing."* By Maria Kondo.

This New York Times best-seller was written by the most popular home organizer in Japan, who has been called "the warrior princess in the war on clutter."

✓ If you want to offer your services as a professional home organizer, read *"How to Start a Home-Based professional Organizing Business."* By Dawn Noble. All three books are available at Amazon.com.

House sitting. Many of your senior clients will travel frequently, from one-week getaways to extended stays for several months in a warmer climate during winter months. If they plan to be gone for a month or more, they may want a house sitter living in their home for security reasons, or to care for pets and plants.

While it's not uncommon for a senior concierge to become a house sitter for a client for a month or two, a more typical arrangement would be to locate a person or couple to do the house sitting for your client. Start by checking online services like www.trustedhousesitters.com, www.housecarers.com or www.mindmyhouse.com.

Most house sitter referral services provide pre-screened sitters. If the service does not, you'll need to have an outside firm do a background check. Simply enter "background check" in your computer search bar to get a list of several.

Be sure to find out your client's expectations for the house sitter. What chores are they expected to do – yard cleanup or mowing, window washing, pet care? – and include that in the agreement that the house sitter signs. If the information is complex, such as a medication schedule for a sick pet, get detailed instructions and the contact information for their veterinarian. The pet sitting agreement in chapter 5 covers all the bases.

Pricing for house sitting depends both on location and responsibilities. A short-term house sitter in a large city like New York or San Francisco would expect around $50 a day, while in smaller cities, the rates could be just $30 a day.

For extended stays – over a month – the house sitters receive free rent as compensation for house sitting. If there is additional work involved, such as caring for cats and dogs, the price should reflect that.

You'll find two useful forms that can be adapted for house sitting in the forms chapter further on in the guide. One is a key release form and the other is a pet sitting agreement.

If your clients don't feel a live-in house sitter is required for day-to-day care of their home while they are gone, offer to do a regular house check, covered earlier in this chapter. Most house checks are done once, twice or three times a week, depending on what the client wants.

Meal preparation. As seniors become less physically active, their appetite decreases. The sense of taste and smell also tend to fade as we age. As a result, many seniors may not be eating a healthy, balanced diet, which can cause a decline in their health and zest for life.

In addition, grocery shopping may be difficult if a senior has mobility problems. Cooking may also be more of a challenge, especially when cooking for just one person. If your senior client seems to have a lack of appetite, or enthusiasm for eating, or has difficulty preparing meals, suggest that someone else help with the meal planning and preparation.

If you love to cook, that someone else could be you. Being a personal chef doesn't have to be a full-time job, as you can spend a half-day preparing a week's worth of delicious, nutritious meals and freeze or refrigerate most of them. For recipe ideas, just do a Google search for "healthy senior meals."

Another lower-cost option is to find a home delivery meal program in your area. The largest and best known is Meals-on-Wheels, but there are many other local programs that deliver hot meals daily or several times a week to seniors who have trouble preparing meals for themselves.

Most programs also accommodate special needs, such as diabetic, low-sodium, Kosher or vegetarian. To help your senior client find a local program, visit www.mealcall.org or www.eldercare.gov.

Online research. According to a recent study by the Pew Research Center, 4 in 10 American seniors never use the internet. The primary reason, aside from health issues and physical challenges such as vision loss, is difficulty in learning and mastering new technology. Of course, 80% of seniors who do regularly go online feel those offline seniors are at a serious advantage.

If your senior clients are not skilled, or just plain scared of using the internet, you can use your computer/internet skills to help make their lives better by teaching them or assisting them in exploring the internet world. Giving them the skills to be confident online can make a huge difference in a senior's life, as it connects them to the outside world in a far bigger way than just watching the evening news on network TV ever will.

A newer, simpler and cheaper way to get them started is to buy a Chromebook. It's easier to use than other computers, which is why it has been embraced by schools around the world. With a Chromebook and an internet connection, seniors can explore the internet, send and receive e-mails, write a novel, or use one of the hundreds of free "apps" that help them explore their specialized interests.

A basic Chromebook, made by well-known computer manufacturers such as HP, Toshiba or Samsung, can be purchased for as little as $250, comes with built-in virus protection that automatically updates for free and browses the web much faster than conventional computers. It's lightweight – most weigh less than 3-pounds – so it's easy to hold in your lap. To learn more, do an online search for "Chromebook reviews."

Here are just a few of the areas you and your senior client can explore on the internet, with you assisting your client, or doing the research for your client:

- Bookmark online websites, based on your client's interests.

- Book shopping online at Amazon.com.

- Compare product ratings at Epinions.com.

- Search for collectibles or crafts at Ebay.com or Etsy.com

- Dating online for seniors, at ourtime.com or match.com/senior.

- Find a capable, trustworthy home repair business at Angieslist.com.

- Research family roots with genealogy research at genealogyintime.com, familysearch.com or genealogy.com.

- Health information online – just pick a topic to search.

- Explore travel options and book lodging and trips.

- Watch a video on any topic at Youtube.com

Pickup & delivery. Seniors appreciate the ease of having items appear at the front door without the hassles of traffic, weather or waiting in lines, and are willing to pay for that convenience. All you need to help them is a reliable vehicle and a cell phone.

Most pickups and deliveries are routine, like a prescription refill, dry cleaning, groceries, or liquor, but the possibilities are limited only by their imagination. One client, an avid gardener, wanted 100 pounds of seaweed washed up on the beach after a winter storm for garden fertilizer. Another client, a retired geologist who needed a very special chunk of rock that required a 120-mile round trip and a pickaxe, paid by the hour plus a mileage charge. Both definitely not your everyday errands!

You'll find the pickup list grows as your clients discover how convenient it is to let you do the fetching. Many clients enjoy a special restaurant meal, but are reluctant or unable to go alone, so they order a meal to go.

Several clients love Costco, so that's a regular pickup with a big list of essentials. Often it's possible to shop for more than one client at the same time and store, like Costco.

To make sure you cover your expenses, be sure to charge a mileage rate for any pickups or deliveries outside your "flat-rate" area, which is a range of about 5-miles in any direction from your client's home. Vehicles wear out, require fuel, maintenance and repairs, so make sure you cover those costs with a mileage charge.

The I.R.S. currently allows a 58 cents per mile deduction for business mileage which is a good starting point for billing your clients. Many concierges use a higher rate – up to double the I.R.S. allowance – for billing.

Pet services. Seniors are spending more and more money each year on their pets and want only the best for their four-legged family members. For pet owners, it makes perfect sense, because pets add so much to our lives, in so many ways. They provide companionship, fun, security and, best of all, unconditional love. Recent medical studies have even shown that our pets can reduce stress and lower blood pressure.

According to a survey of pet owners, most allow their pets to sleep on their bed, celebrate their pet's birthday and include their pets in family photos. Another part of the special attention our pets receive is special care while we're away. No more scary trips to the kennel. Today, pet care pros, such as a pet sitter or senior concierge, are part of a pet's "extended family", ready to pitch in when owners must be away from their pets for a day, a week or longer.

According to a recent National Pet Owner's Survey, conducted by the APPM, 63 percent of U.S. households own a pet, and 45 percent of all households own more than one pet. There are 75 million dogs and 89 million cats in the United States, not to mention birds, (16 million) reptiles, (13 million) small mammals, (24 million) and fish (14 million). That's a lot of pet care!

In the past, pet owners had to send their pets to a kennel or find a willing friend or relative. Today, with your help, or the help of a pet sitter, pets can stay in the familiar and secure surroundings of home. No stressful interactions with strange dogs or cats, no risk of exposure to illnesses in the confines of a kennel, and lots of TLC from a pet sitter. In addition, pet sitters can give a home a "lived in" look during vacations by bringing in mail, turning lights on and off and watering houseplants.

Most pet visits take about a half hour – longer if the dog needs extended walk or there are multiple pets. Make sure your schedule will allow about two hours in the morning and two hours in the afternoon to handle the visits, plus the time it takes to get from one visit to the next.

It's best to fit your pet rounds to your own preferences whenever possible. A "morning person", for example, might start her day with the first visit around 7 a.m., while one who likes a later start might make the same visit at 9 or 10 a.m. Scheduling often revolves around other activities as well, such as getting the kids off to school.

Just Another Pet Care Day!

Our first stop is to visit Annie & Ivy, two cockapoos whose owners are on vacation for two weeks. Like most dogs, they are eager to get outside for a bathroom break when you arrive. Once that's taken care of, they are ready for breakfast and a bit of play time. Then Ivy gets ear drops for an infection, and another five minutes of play time in the back yard. Then it's back in the house, lock up and go. A 5-minute drive brings us to the home of Winston, a sweet pug who treats you like a long-lost friend every time you walk through the door. Winston likes a walk after a quick breakfast, so we take a stroll around the block. Back at the house, a quick check reveals no accidents, water the house plants, and off to visit our next buddy.

Sadie is a corgi whose owners are on a cruise for a few days. Sadie lives in a third-floor condo and has been trained to use a litter box on the balcony. But today, we take the stairs to give her a bit more exercise, and head to a small park across the street, where she greets two dog pals and plays for a few minutes. Then back up the stairs to drop off Sadie, (Did I mention the free pet care fitness program?) a stop at Starbucks for a mid-morning coffee and then a visit with Dusty, a rescue greyhound. Dusty also likes to go out for a morning walk, so today we take her for a 20-minute loop

25

through her neighborhood before heading back to the house. Feed the parakeets, water the house plants, and bring in the mail, then time for a lunch break.

Pet Sitting Tips

✓ Always knock when you arrive at a client's home in case a relative or friend is visiting, or they have arrived home early. No surprises!

✓ Don't help the burglars! This means not doing anything that would signal that the owners are away. Always keep a supply of business cards handy just in case a suspicious neighbor calls the police during your visit.

✓ Always keep the house key attached to your body with an elastic wrist band or belt clip. It's so embarrassing to set the key on the kitchen counter while you're feeding the dog, take the dog in the back yard to play, and have the wind blow the door shut (and locked!) It happens more often than you might think!

✓ Take a walk around the house during every visit to check for accidents that may need cleaning up or anything out of the ordinary.

✓ Many clients will also request "house sitting" services as well, such as bringing in the mail, turning lights on and off and watering plants. These minor chores can be done in the course of a regular visit and should be included in the basic charge unless they take a lot of extra time.

✓ To prevent pets from running away or getting lost, ask your clients if there is a fenced or secure area for their pet. Also make sure pets have and ID tag/collar to help if they do go astray. It's also important to protect yourself with a clause in your service agreement that releases you from liability if a pet gets away and is lost, injured or dies.

✓ Don't let anyone else in a client's home unless you have written authorization from the customer. This includes repairmen and neighbors. The only exception is emergency personnel, such as firemen or police.

✓ Get all your instructions in writing – that's why having a signed service agreement is important – to prevent any misunderstandings.

✓ Be very careful if you've been asked to water plants while pet sitting. Make sure no water spills on the floors or furniture, as water damage is one of the most common reasons for an insurance claim.

✓ Ask your customers how they want accidents cleaned up. They will often have a favorite product to use. Even if they claim their pet never has accidents, explain that pets can get upset when owners leave, and express their mood with a change in potty behavior!

✓ Cats always want their food first, but you will encounter a few shy cats that tend to go into hiding when you arrive. Talk to your customer at your get acquainted meeting about their pet's favorite hiding places, if this is a problem.

✓ Many pets – and their owners – have special rituals that you'll need to attend to, such as grooming or treats. Many cats, for example, refuse to drink water from a bowl, so you'll need to make sure there is a slowly dripping faucet for them. One memorable basset hound would start howling if his favorite country-western station wasn't turned on!

✓ It's a good idea to get two keys from customers – one for a backup and one for daily use. Test them on your get acquainted visit to make sure they work. If you only have one key, make sure you get the name and emergency contact information for someone in the area who also has a house key.

✓ If your customer has an alarm system, get the entry codes and the name and phone number of the alarm company.

✓ Use a color code or numbering system on your key tags to keep the key and the owner's information separate. This will prevent problems if the keys are lost or stolen.

✓ Hand deliver the house keys when your client returns. This is safer than leaving them hidden at their house and gives you an opportunity to get paid. You'll find many customers prefer that you keep a key for future assignments, as this saves them time and fees.

✓ Take a minute to leave a note after each visit, sharing little tidbits about how their dog or cat did today (appetite, mood, etc.)

Other Pet Care Services

Dog Walking. Clients with mobility issues often need someone to take their dog for a daily walk. It' easy, fun, profitable and good exercise. Dog walking rates are based on the time you need to properly exercise a dog – puppies and active breeds take more time, while older dogs and less active breeds take less.

Pet Transportation. Clients may not always be available to transport their pets to and from vet appointments, the groomer or to pick up pet supplies. This is an ideal add-on task, with rates usually set on an hourly or half-hourly basis plus mileage.

Overnight Pet Sitting. Customers will often ask if you can provide this service. If your schedule is flexible, overnighting can be a profitable sideline.

Horse Sitting. If you live in the country and are familiar with horse care, this is a specialized type of pet sitting you may enjoy. After all, horse owners take vacations too, and can't always count on a friend or relative to help out. Get the word out through local horse clubs and with a notice on the bulletin board at your local feed store.

Relocation assistance. There comes a time in every senior's life when they must move because they no longer live alone or care for themselves. A senior concierge or a senior move manager can smooth the way during this stressful time of life.

As our nation ages, the number of elders who need to move to a senior living facility has soared, and the demand for folks who are able to help with this difficult transition has grown dramatically. For example, the number of members in the National Association of Senior Move Managers has grown from just 30 to over 800 since 2002.

The average age of a senior who is moving from their home to a senior living facility is 84. As you might imagine, someone that age is not likely to be packing and moving themselves. They need help – with packing, moving and counseling. Helping clients deal with the stresses of moving – and leaving their old life behind – is a huge part of the process, and those who can also provide effective support to their client's emotional needs will do well.

Most senior concierges enjoy helping their senior clients relocate, as the job takes both organizational skills and people skills. Here are the six steps in a typical senior move:

Floor planning. Measure the new home, room by room and create a floor plan, either on graph paper or by using room planning software. Whether you use a laptop or a tablet, there are dozens of easy-to-use, mostly free, room planning programs available. To see what is currently available, do an online search for "room planner." After drawing the new floor plan, have a chat with your client about which furniture they would like to bring along, measure each piece, and draw that on the floor plan to make sure it will fit.

Downsize. With your client's help, go through the house one room at a time, including every closet, cabinet and the attic and garage. Using color coded sticky dots or a list, divide everything into three groups: Items to keep and move, items to be given to family and friends and items to be sold or given away.

Timetable. Set up a moving timetable, and coordinate that with the client, their family, the staff at the new home and the packers and movers. Set up a time for a garage or estate sale to dispose of all the items in group 3.

Packing. Pack all items to be moved. You can hire pros or work with your client and their family during the packing. Be careful in this phase to always charge by the hour, whether you're packing or supervising, as the more family members are involved, the longer it will take – guaranteed!

Moving day. Time for the final packing of last-minute items. This is often a very emotional time for your client, so be sure to make time to offer emotional support, and all the TLC they might need. Supervise the movers to make sure everything goes smoothly.

New home – unpack. Even if your client is there, you'll need to help the movers arrange the furniture and place boxes, help your client unpack boxes, remove the boxes and all packing material, put things away in closets, cabinets and furniture. To make your client's life a little less stressful, it's best if you make the beds, set up the kitchen, connect the telephone, TV and lamps and hang any pictures on the walls.

Running errands. Providing a list of services you offer to seniors in a flyer or on a website will help generate calls and assignments. Don't worry about being too specific with your list. Just cover the general services you plan to offer, and add a line at the end, such as: *"Don't see what you're looking for? Call us to discuss your needs."*

Here are the most common services requested by seniors:

Banking errands. Homebound seniors often need help with their banking needs, such as making deposits or getting cash.

Car errands. When it's time for an oil change, repairs, or just a trip to the car wash, you can help.

Dry cleaning. Many dry cleaners don't offer a pick-up and delivery service, but you can.

General errands. Prepare to be surprised by some of the errand requests you'll get. Most will be routine, such as dropping off books at the library or purchasing stamps at the post office.

Grocery shopping. This is one of the most popular services, as many seniors are homebound, and unable to get to the grocery store. You'll find helpful forms to cover grocery shopping in the forms chapter.

Personal shopping. You may be asked to shop for anything, from auto parts to pet toys.

Prescriptions. Most pharmacies do not deliver, so you can help seniors get their medications.

Transportation. For many seniors who want to stay independent as long as possible, transportation is the largest challenge to their independence. Some are unable to drive a vehicle, while others may be facing a temporary situation, such as recovering from surgery, that prevents them from getting behind the wheel.

Seniors who choose not to drive, or are not able to drive, depend on family, friends or public transportation for help in getting around. But there are times when none of these free options are available, and that is where private senior transportation comes to the rescue with service when and where it is needed.

Providing safe, reliable transportation for seniors, with a caring driver who can wait for them at doctor visits or help them get around at a visit to a store, is always in demand. It is one of the best services a senior concierge can offer.

Unless you plan to buy a specialized van to transport those who need a wheelchair ramp or lift, which is quite expensive, just offer transportation services to your more able clients. Clients who can get in and out of their wheelchairs with a little help should be the focus in offering a basic senior transportation service as part of your concierge services, and you can refer clients who need a ramp or lift to other service providers in your area.

If you decide to offer senior transportation as part of your concierge service, be sure to check with your state department of licensing or transportation to find out if there are any restrictions for a senior transportation service.

Your insurance company will also likely require that you purchase commercial liability insurance or other additional insurance coverage. How you charge can often make a difference in your insurance and licensing requirements, so it may be best to charge by the hour for your time, and not by the mile.

Travel planning. Seniors, especially those with limited or no computer skills, often need help planning a trip or booking transportation and rooms. Even for those of us who are used to navigating the online world, the huge number of travel sites can take hours to explore and locate what you want.

Offering travel planning & booking help may actually save your client money, as you can find discounts that can knock a big percentage off the total trip cost. Here are a few tips to help your clients save money on their next trip:

- ✓ Use a "fare aggregator" like Kayak.com, which scans hundreds of web sites to find the cheapest airfares. Also check fares at Southwest.com, for budget fares within the U.S.

- ✓ Avoid peak travel days and save big. For example, a flight on Tuesday, Wednesday or Saturday afternoon is almost always cheaper. A free online tool call Trip Starter at Hotwire.com can also show you the cheapest dates and times to fly. Overall, expect to save 15% to 20% using these free online tools.

- ✓ Go off-season to save on accommodations and packages in areas that have lots of peak season visitors. Online travel agencies, such as Expedia.com, Orbitz.com and Travelocity. com always have great bargains on complete travel packages to well-known destinations in the off-season.

✓ Cruise for less. Cruises are popular among seniors, so book smart to save a lot. Start by visiting CruiseCompete. com, where you can list your cruise preferences and get competing bids from several cruise agencies.

✓ Two other tried and true methods for cheaper cruising are to book at the last minute and book a "repositioning" cruise. At the end of the season, cruise ships relocate their ships to warmer areas, such as Alaska in the summer, then to Baja in the winter. To check for current repositioning deals, visit CruiseCompete.com

You'll need to sit down with your client and explore their travel preferences and goals. Once you have that basic information, you and your client can find the best options for their next trip. When the choices are narrowed down to the best one, you can help them by making the actual reservations online or suggesting a trained travel consultant for the job. Here are the questions you need to ask before starting your online research:

1. Domestic or foreign travel?
2. Special interests, such as a specific region, cities, museums or historical sites?
3. Active or relaxed – such as a walking tour of Rome or a Mediterranean cruise?
4. When would your client prefer to travel?
5 Escorted tour or independent travel?
6. Budget for the trip?

If you find travel planning for your clients enjoyable, you may want to affiliate with an agency to earn a commission for your efforts, or at the very least, a referral fee. Agencies that work with part-timers such as concierges are called "host agencies." You can locate those in your state at the website of the National Association of Commissioned Travel Agents: www.nacta.com/host_list.

Vehicle services. When a senior is unable to drive their vehicle, someone still has to take it to the repair shop, the car wash or the Jiffy Lube for service. Some clients are temporarily sidelined due to a health issue, and others may never drive again, but are not willing to sell their car or truck.

Waiting service. Last year, according to a national survey, Americans wasted 2.75 billion – yes, billion – hours waiting for in-home services, such as a furnace repair, furniture delivery or the cable guy. The most waited-for service: cable and satellite TV, followed by internet providers, then appliance and computer repairmen.

At a more local level, you can help your senior clients when they can't be there for an in-home service call. Just let them know you're available to wait at their home when they are away, until the repairman shows up and the work is done. While you're waiting, you may be able to complete a chore or two on the client's to-do list, or simply read a book while you relax and wait.

CHAPTER TWO

Setting Up Your Senior Concierge Service

Before you can legally start your new business, there are several steps you'll need to complete. Here are the basic requirements:

- Choose your legal form of business.

- Pick a business name.

- Obtain a tax ID number and business licenses.

- Business insurance.

- Set up a bank account.

- Set up a record-keeping system.

Most senior concierges are "lone eagles," and prefer to keep their business small and simple. Others, attracted to the higher income potential, hire employees to do most of the actual work and focus on managing the business.

While it's true a larger senior concierge service can generate a substantial income, there is a lot of work involved. You have to hire and manage employees, handle endless administrative tasks, and spend less time out and about, actually helping senior clients. It's up to you to decide which direction to take.

Legal form of business. If you intend to have no employees, a sole proprietorship makes sense. If you envision two or more partners, a partnership or limited liability corporation (LLC) could be a good choice. Most new small businesses are choosing the LLC format, as it's easy to set up (most states have free downloadable forms) and does not require a separate tax return to be filed.

Sole Proprietorship. The easiest legal form of business to set up but has limited legal protection. The business operates under your personal social security number, and federal taxes are paid as part of your 1040 tax return.

Limited Liability Corporation (LLC). Popular because owners have limited personal liability, management flexibility and pass-through taxation (taxes are also paid as a part of your standard 1040 return.

To learn more about choosing the best legal structure for your new senior concierge business, visit www.nolo.com, and click on "free legal information." Nolo can also help you properly establish a limited liability corporation in any state.

Pick a Business Name

Start by making a list of several possible business names that best describe your new senior concierge company. Be sure to pick a name that suggests what your company is all about, as that name is the first impression a prospective client will have.

For example, Dependable Senior Concierge Service tells a prospect what you do as well as suggesting that your company is dependable. Adding the name of your town tells prospects your service area, as well as make it easier for the search engines, such as Google, to find your web site when you set that up. Here are a few ideas to get you started:

- ✓ At Your Service
- ✓ Mission Accomplished
- ✓ Leisure for You
- ✓ On the Run for You
- ✓ There When You Can't Be
- ✓ One Call Does It All
- ✓ "Your Town" Senior Concierge

Be sure to choose a name that is easy to spell and remember. Before you make your final selection, get feedback from family or friends. Do they like it? Could it be improved?

After you've chosen a name, verify that you can use the name. Start by checking to see if the name can be registered as a domain name, as you'll need a website containing your company name to help customers and prospects contact you online and learn more about your services. You can get a free domain name when you sign up for web site hosting at BlueHost.

I've used BlueHost for years, and have always been pleased with their service, especially the 24/7 telephone help, with U.S. based customer service folks.

Next, check with your county clerk's office to see if your proposed business name is in use by anyone else. If you plan to use an LLC legal structure, check with your state's corporate filing office or Secretary of State.

Do a federal trademark search (free, at USPTO.gov) of the name you've chosen to ensure no one else is using the name, or if your use of the name would confuse someone, or if the name is "famous."

Now that you've made sure your chosen business name is available, it's time to register the name. In most cases, this is handled by your local county clerk's office.

File for Licenses and Permits

Start with the IRS, as you'll need the "Employer Identification Number," or EIN, when you apply for other licenses, permits and a bank account. Visit the IRS web site at www.irs.gov and enter "Form SS4" in the search window.

Next, you can choose to print the application form, or apply online. Applying online is much faster, and you can actually get your EIN when you've finished filling out the form!

After you have the EIN, apply for a local (city or county) business license. They may ask how many employees you intend to have. If you plan to use a home office, they are concerned about traffic and parking issues. Just tell them that customers or employees, if any, will never visit the office – it is only for management work, such as bookkeeping.

Some states may require a special home care license and registration if you perform what they consider senior non-medical home care services. When this book was updated last, only 28 of the 50 states require a special license for home care businesses. Check with your state to find out the specific requirements and if your concierge business may require state licensing. Here's a list of who to contact in each state:

- Alabama Dept. of Human Resources: www.dhr.state.al.us

- Alaska Dept. of Health & Social Services: www.hss.state.ak.us

- Arizona Dept. of Economic Security: www.azdes.gov

- Arkansas Dept. of Human Services: www.humanservices.arkansas.gov

- California Dept. of Social Services: www.dss.cahwnet.gov

- Colorado Dept. of Human Services: www.cdhs.state.co.us

- Connecticut Dept. of Social Services: www.ct.gov/dss/site/default.asp

- Delaware Dept. of Health & Social Services: www.dhss.delaware.gov/dhss

- District of Columbia Dept. of Human Services: www.dhs.dc.gov

- Florida Agency for Health Care Admin:
  www.fdhc.state.fl.us

- Georgia Dept. of Human Services:
  www.dhr.state.ga.us

- Hawaii Dept. of Human Services:
  www.hawaii.gov/dhs

- Idaho Dept. of Health & Welfare:
  www.healthandwelfare.idaho.gov

- Illinois Dept. of Human Services:
  www.dhs.state.il.us

- Indiana Family & Social Services:
  www.in.gov/fssa

- Iowa Dept. of Human Services:
  www.dhs.state.ia.us

- Kansas Dept. of Social & Rehabilitation Services:
  www.dcf.ks.gov

- Kentucky Dept of Health & Human Services:
  www.chfs.ky.gov

- Louisiana Dept. of Social Services:
  www.dss.state.la.us

- Maine Dept. of Health & Human Services:
  www.maine.gov/dhhs

- Maryland Dept. of Human Resources:
  www.dhr.state.md.us

- Massachusetts Dept. of Social Services: www.mass.gov/dss

- Michigan Dept. of Community Health: www.michigan.gov/mdch

- Minnesota Dept. of Human Services: www.dhs.state.mn.us

- Mississippi Dept. of Human Services: www.mdhs.state.ms.us

- Missouri Dept. of Social Services: www.dss.mo.gov

- Montana Dept. of Health & Human Services: www.dphhs.mt.gov

- Nebraska Health & Human Services: www.dhhs.ne.gov

- Nevada Dept. of Human Resources: www.dhhs.nv.gov

- New Hampshire Dept. of Health & Human Services: www.dhhs.state.nh.us

- New Jersey Dept. of Human Services: www.state.nj.us/humanservices

- New Mexico Health & Human Services: www.hsd.state.nm.us

- New York State Family Services: www.homecare.nyhealth.gov

- North Carolina Dept. of Health & Human Services:
  www.dhhs.state.nc.us

- North Dakota Dept. of Human Services:
  www.dhs.nd.gov

- Ohio Dept. of Family Services:
  www.jfs.ohio.gov

- Oklahoma Dept. of Family Services:
  www.okdhs.org

- Oregon Dept. of Human Services:
  www.oregon.gov/DHS

- Pennsylvania Dept. of Public Welfare:
  www.dpw.state.pa.us

- Rhode Island Dept. of Human Services:
  www.dhs.ri.gov

- South Carolina Dept. of Health & Human Services:
  www.scdhhs.gov

- Tennessee Dept. of Human Services:
  www.state.tn.us/humanserv

- Texas Health & Human Services:
  www.hhsc.state.tx.us

- Utah Dept. of Human Services:
  www.dhs.state.ut.us

- Vermont Agency of Human Services:
  www.humanservices.vermont.gov

- Virginia Dept. of Social Services: www.dss.state.va.us

- Washington Dept. of Social & health Services: www.dshs.wa.gov

- West Virginia Dept. of Health & Human Resources: www.dhhr.wv.gov

- Wisconsin Dept. of Health & Family Services: www.dhs.wisconsin.gov

- Wyoming Dept. of Health: www.health.wyo.gov/aging

Business Insurance

Business insurance provides financial protection for your new senior concierge business. When you are providing services in client's homes, almost anything can, and will, happen, but you can make sure any potential liability is covered by an insurance umbrella. Working with an insurance broker is usually advised, as they can provide quotes from several companies for the different types of insurance you will need.

General Liability. This type of insurance covers damage to a client's property, libel and slander, slip and fall claims and other risks.

Non-Owned Auto Liability. If an employee causes an at-fault accident while driving on the job, you're covered. For example, if you are driving a client to a doctor's appointment and hit a pedestrian.

Professional Liability. For a senior concierge service, this insurance covers damages from improper care or absence of proper care. For example, a fall while assisting a client up the stairs, or a fall because you were not helping the client down the stairs while at their home.

Workmen's Compensation. This insurance is mandatory in 49 states and covers on-the-job injuries. This insurance protects employers from lawsuits caused by workplace accidents and provides compensation for lost income and medical care to employees injured in workplace accidents or caused by work related illnesses.

Most states have a government sponsored plan, which is usually cheaper than private workman's compensation insurance. If your state does not, always get at least two quotes for this insurance.

When you're getting started, you will be asked to estimate your payroll to determine the insurance premium. It is generally best to use a low estimate until you have actual numbers, as your initial deposit is based on the estimate.

While you may have heard it's best to classify your employees as "independent contractors" to avoid workman's compensation insurance, don't do it unless they have an actual business license and insurance.

The I.R.S. and the courts have tough standards for determining whether a person is an employee or an independent contractor. The courts call it the "right to control" test. If the hiring person controls the way the work is carried out, such as hours worked or which client to visit, the relationship between the parties is employer/employee.

An additional test: if a person depends on a business for steady income, they are an employee. If the employer has no authority over how a person does their work, that person could be an independent contractor.

Taxes & Accounting

There are three types of taxes you'll be responsible for as a business owner, employment taxes, income tax and self-employment tax. If you do not have employees, you generally do not have to pay employment taxes, but just a self-employment tax.

It's a good idea to visit a tax pro, such as an accountant, to learn just what taxes will be required for the type of business you plan to start. They can also advise you what information they will require to help you at tax time, such as a profit and loss statement.

To keep accounting costs low, you should do as much as possible yourself. Today, most accounting software for small businesses has gone online, and is called "cloud" software, as it is web-hosted rather than from a program installed on your computer. This allows the software company to easily update programs to reflect changes in tax laws and other regulations.

A small senior concierge business does not need a high-powered, expensive accounting system, but something that is simple enough to be easy to understand and use. It should also be capable of generating invoices for your clients, and reports needed by your accountant or tax professional. It's up to you to choose the best one for you. Here are my current favorites:

Fresh Books. This cloud-based accounting program is considered one of the best invoicing solutions available, which is important for any senior service business with dozens of clients to bill regularly. It even includes time-tracking, so you can easily add billable time to an invoice. You can also add auto-billing and automatic payment reminders and thank you notes!

Like most, they offer a free trial period so new users can see if they like the program before spending any money. Their pricing is based on the number of clients you invoice. Because it is web-based, there are no downloads or installations, and it is compatible with all operating systems as long as you have internet access.

Fresh Books is very easy to use, a big plus for a non-accountant like me (and you?) The setup is simple and quick, and the interface is easy to figure out and logical. Help is available online and by phone. When I call, the waiting time is under 2 minutes.

GoDaddy Bookkeeping. This software, formerly called Outright, is more user-friendly than most accounting programs. It's more of a bookkeeping program aimed at small businesses that just need to account for income, expenses and taxes.

The company was started by two guys who worked at Intuit, the parent company of Quickbooks, to offer a simpler solution for small business owners who didn't know much about accounting but needed to have accurate data for their taxes.

This software is also cloud-based, so there are no downloads, and you can access your account anywhere you have an internet connection, even on your iPad or smartphone. The cost is quite affordable – currently about $100 per year.

Like all the other cloud accounting programs, you can link your accounts, such as bank accounts, credit cards, PayPal and even your eBay seller account. Then it automatically downloads the information daily. Of course, it can create and send invoices to customers, and has a great built-in time sheet, so you can track billable hours to a specific client and send an invoice based on those hours.

Unlike most of the other online programs, there is no extra charge for additional clients. Whether you have two clients or two hundred, the cost is the same. To learn more, visit: www.outright.com

Quickbooks Online. Everyone has heard of Quicken, which has been available since the mid-80s, followed by Quickbooks. It is the Big Dog of accounting software and used by thousands of companies.

Quickbooks Online has a 3-tier pricing plan, and a 30-day free trial. The basic "Simple Start" plan includes invoicing and estimates, as well as all the normal accounting features. The "Essentials" plan adds an accounts payable function to track and pay bills. The "Plus" plan allows subscribers to track inventory and generate 1099 forms.

The software is web-hosted, so no downloads or installation is required, and is compatible with Windows and Mac OS X operating systems. Setup is easy and quick and includes several how-to videos. There are a huge numbers of features available to users, but the less-used ones are kept in the background for regular users.

Because it is more complex than the other programs I've mentioned, there are a few challenges, and a steeper learning curve. For example, when you send an invoice, it automatically includes a "Pay Now" button, which requires you to use the Quicken electronic payment system. Guess what? That system is more costly than other options, such as PayPal.

Another problem is poor support. Long wait times for phone support are common, and online support is spotty. This could improve however, so check a few online reviews before signing on with them. Do a web search for "QuickBooks online community forum" to find out what others currently think.

Business Plan

Although many business experts insist that a business plan is essential to starting a small business, that's not always true. For every business that fails because of poor planning, there are five that never succeed because of too much planning. As the great Michael Jordan said, "Just do it!"

The secret of a successful senior concierge business is providing the services that people want to buy. A business plan can't tell you that, but real customers can. Instead of wasting a lot of time and energy coming up with a business plan, just start talking to your potential customers to find out what they need and figure out how to give it to them.

Regardless of how much planning you do, it's only a hunch – an educated guess about how well your business will do. The danger is, by spending too much time on planning, you'll have less energy/time/money to try new ideas. The secret is to test your ideas as quickly and cheaply as possible, then improve and refine them.

And speaking of cheap & quick, here's a way to do a very simple business plan for your new senior concierge business. If you plan to borrow money from a relative or friend – the most common source of funding for small startup businesses – do an "executive summary" business plan to show them you've done your homework.

It should cover just the business plan basics, with an overview of the business, a market analysis with a look at your competition, and an estimate of your first year's sales. It assumes that you will not have employees or buying or leasing property or equipment. Here's a sample:

AT YOUR SERVICE – SENIOR CONCIERGE BUSINESS PLAN

- **Business Overview:** At Your Service is a new senior concierge service based in Bend, Oregon, specializing in seniors. The business will cover the greater Bend area. Our customers are seniors who need a variety of services to remain independent.

- **Market Analysis:** The demand for reliable, cost-effective senior concierge services has been growing in the area for several years as the town's senior population continues to grow. There are only two other local senior concierge services in the area, and we believe there is ample room, due to our growing senior population, for another reliable senior service.

- **Marketing Strategy:** The marketing strategy of At Your Service – Senior Concierge is to provide dependable and exceptional services to seniors and their out-of-town children who have a regular need for concierge services. This will ensure that the business will have a regular, steady income from repeat customers. The second part of our marketing strategy will be to gain customers who need concierge services occasionally, such as anyone recovering from an illness or surgery, or those who are unable to leave home for other medical reasons.

- **First Year Goal:** Based on the size of the local senior market and the fact that At Your Service Senior Concierge will be a one-person business, our sales projection for the first year is $60,000. We plan to build our customer base through direct contact with prospective customers and word-of-mouth referrals from happy customers to continue to grow our service as demand grows.

Free Help to Start Your New Business

There is a free resource available to help start-up companies, including senior concierge businesses. SCORE is a government program that taps the experience and brainpower of retired business owners to help new owners get off to a successful start. If you find you need a comprehensive business plan to get funding for your new courier business, SCORE can help you with that as well. To find the nearest office, visit: score.org.

Once you have picked a business name and checked to make sure no one else has claimed the name, you can print your business cards, flyers and forms. Check with local suppliers, such as your favorite office supply store, or online printers, like www.gotprint.net, www.psprint.com,www.uprinting.com and www.vistaprint.com.

Setting Fees

The fees for your senior concierge service depend on your local market. If you live in a small town, you will earn less than a concierge doing the very same tasks in a big city. That may not seem fair, but higher fees in the city are needed to pay for things like expensive parking, rent and other services.

The first step in setting your hourly fees is to do an internet search for concierge services in your area to see what others are charging. This gives you a general guideline of what you may be able to charge. Also keep in mind that a senior concierge charges less than a concierge who specializes in helping busy executives.

The work of a senior concierge is usually not as demanding, and, to be honest, most seniors don't have the high income of a corporate executive to be able to afford premium fees.

It is best to have one hourly rate for your services, rather than several, to avoid confusing your senior clients. Another approach that works for many concierges is to find out the rates for specialized services, such as managing a senior relocation, then quoting a specific rate for that service if the need arises.

It's best to set a minimum for your work, so your clients know they need to have enough tasks to keep you busy for that time, say two hours, for example. You can specify that in your service contract. It's also a good idea to leave a printed notepad with your name and phone number so your clients can make a list of tasks for you before they call, to ensure there is enough work for your minimum.

Package Pricing & Surcharges

Many senior concierge services offer a "package" to their regular customers. It's a win-win, as you get paid up front and know in advance how many hours you'll be booked. Your customers save a bit (10 percent is the standard "package" discount) as well.

One service offers a "gold" package for $100 a month that covers two grocery shopping trips, two pharmacy trips and two general errands. The "diamond" package, for $180, adds four more hours per month.

You can also offer a basic discount package, priced by the total number of hours. For example:

$110 – Up to 5 hours per month.

$175 – Up to 8 hours per month.

$220 – Up to 10 hours per month.

Another option is offering your regular customers a ten percent discount if they exceed a certain number of hours each month.

Surcharges

The normal hours for a senior concierge service are 8 a.m. to 6 p.m., with 24-hour notice to allow you to schedule each day in advance. If a customer needs your help after hours or during a holiday, a surcharge is customary. Typical surcharges are:

- After hours during the work week or anytime on weekends - $6 per hour additional.
- Holiday service - $10 per hour additional.
- Rush service (within 2-4 hours) $10 per hour additional.

Be sure to mention the additional charges when your customer calls or include it in your flyer, brochure or service agreement. If you don't charge extra, expect frequent requests for help late in the day, on holidays or on short notice.

It's customary to request that your customers schedule a project 24 hours ahead. This gives you the ability to organize your schedule for efficiency, as well as the possibility of combining trips to save your customers some money. Most senior concierge services request 24-hour notice to cancel, with a cancellation fee if notice is not given. If you plan to do this, be sure to mention it is your policy sheet. Some charge a flat fee and others simply use the rate for one hour of service as a cancellation fee.

Scheduling

To make money as a senior concierge, you have to use your time efficiently and stay organized. You also need to set goals for your own personal work schedule in order to avoid being on call 24/7 for your clients.

Most senior clients are not demanding and understand that you have a life too. The best approach in balancing your life with your client's needs is to explain that you try to keep a schedule, and your hours are 9 a.m. to 3 p.m. (or whatever hours work best for you.)

Life is unpredictable, of course, so you'll need to be flexible enough to accommodate those last-minute requests or emergencies your clients will have. After all, that's why they are paying you! Fortunately, many of the tasks can be handled with a phone call or email.

Using an online scheduling program or calendar can really simplify your record-keeping, whether it's three clients or two dozen to track. Here are a few options for a small senior concierge business:

- **Appointy.com** This free service works with Google Calendar, also free.

- **Setmore.com** Another free service, which allows up to 20 employees and unlimited appointments.

- **GoDaddy.com** Their bookkeeping service, mentioned earlier, includes free scheduling and invoicing as part of the package. Just click on the total hours, and an invoice is generated, ready to send to your client. You can even set up automatic reminders for late payers!

- **Google Calendar** If you are doing your own billing, just download the free calendar from Google (www.google.com/calendar) to schedule and track your hours and appointments.

Getting Paid – Cash, Check or Credit Card?

Most of your customers will be regulars, who use your services over and over again. If they are occasional or first-time users, it's best to get paid at the completion of each project.

Frequent customers – those who use your service often – should have the option of paying weekly or monthly. To do this, you'll need to keep an accurate log of your time, with customer names, start and end times and mileage, if any, for each job and a list of any items purchased or out-of-pocket expenses. This can be transferred to a written receipt or invoice for your customers.

Don't forget to keep a mileage log, so you can also have a record for your tax return, as the I.R.S. currently allows a 58 cents per mile deduction for business mileage.

A simple receipt or invoice book and a rubber stamp with your business information (available at any office supply store) will work while you're getting started. After a while, you may find doing invoices on your computer is more efficient.

If you're dealing with a new customer, you may want to get a deposit. Seniors are generally honest folks, so you won't have many problems with payments. The only issue that may occasionally come up is forgetfulness – the well-known "senior moment." As a few of your customers, due to their advanced age, get a bit absent minded, you may need to remind them if a bill goes unpaid too long.

If you set up discount packages for your regular customers, collect the full amount in advance of the month of use. Keep track of your hours, and if they go over the number of hours in the package, add the extra time to the next month's bill.

If you provide grocery shopping services, you'll want to get paid on delivery. Be sure to inform your grocery shopping customers what form of payment you expect. The grocery shopping form, in a later chapter, will help prevent any misunderstanding.

Another option often used with regular customers is to set up a purchase account for any amount you and your customer agree on. If it's just used for occasional purchases, $100 might be fine, while groceries will require more. When the balance gets low, have your customer add to the account when you run the next errand for them. This method requires more bookkeeping but could save you time in collecting payments for shopping if your customer happens to be away when you deliver the items.

If you are working directly with a client who is paying the bills, ask them what payment method they would prefer. Many seniors are a bit old-fashioned and prefer to use cash or a check to pay.

Many clients rely on their adult children, who may live far away, to pay their bills. For them, as well as seniors paying their own bills with a credit or debit card, you should offer a way to accept a charge card. I recommend using a credit card processor that does not charge a monthly fee as that can cut into your profits. Two companies that I recommend (and use regularly), cater to small businesses, and charge affordable rates:

PayPal. This company is the largest online payment processor in the world, yet still offers excellent customer service. Your clients can easily pay their bill, and the payment goes directly to your account., where you can access it with a debit card, or transfer it to your bank account. www.paypal.com

ProPay. Using the ProPay credit card reader on your smart phone you can swipe a client's credit or debit card on the spot or enter their credit card information online. www.propay.com

Run Your Senior Concierge Business with Just a Phone

Just a few years ago, smartphones did not exist. Today, a smartphone packs far more computing power than the computers used to put a man on the moon! Now almost everything you need to run your senior concierge service – from scheduling to billing to getting paid on the go – can be done from your smartphone or tablet.

Running a small service business means that you must wear many hats. You are the CEO (Chief Everything Officer) of your business, so whatever needs to get done falls right on your shoulders.

Fortunately for you, there's an app for everything you need to get done, and it's available free or for a very low cost at the app store. Using the right apps can help you deliver great customer service, keep a tight and profitable schedule and win the hearts of your customers.

As your senior concierge business grows, you'll need to keep track of customer schedules days in advance, keep track of each customer's special needs, and make sure you get paid by your private pay customers, whether they have cash or a credit card.

To help you do all that with the most productivity and the least hassle, let's take a look at the best apps for your senior concierge service.

Scheduling Your Jobs

A great calendar is almost as good as having your own personal assistant to help keep your days flowing smoothly so you can make more money. Without a calendar app on your smartphone, you might forget appointments and have unhappy customers.

Since your smartphone already comes with a built-in calendar app, so why not use that one? Simply because there are other alternative calendar apps that do a better job, especially for this specific business.

They are fast and easy to use, so you don't waste time searching for what you need. The best apps have a simple, uncluttered look, so checking it several times a day will be a pleasant experience, not a frustrating one.

The two most widely used calendar apps that are pre-installed on either any Android phone or the iPhone are Google Calendar and Apple Calendar. Both have a lot going for them, including the ability to connect to your calendar across multiple devices, like your computer, tablet or smartphone.

Google Calendar allows you to keep several calendars, so you can separate personal and work schedules, and allows you to color-code entries to make it easy to find a specific item. You can also use it to search your contact file or Gmail account.

Apple Calendar is built into every iPhone, and syncs with all other Apple devices. The clean and simple design makes it easier to use than Google Calendar. For example, tapping the + sign creates a new event, like a new customer and their schedule.

Now let's take a look at the other calendar apps that might be better for you. My personal favorite for iPhone users is Fantastical 2, by Flexbits. It's incredibly easy to use, fast and powerful. When you look at your day's events, they are all readable and easy to understand. You can add new events with just a few taps, and even view your schedule in 3 modes to allow you to view days, weeks or months. The cost is around $5 at the Apple app store.

If you have an Android phone, my favorite choice for upgrading is called Business Calendar, by Appgenix software. The interface is simply amazing – you almost feel it was custom designed just for your business.

Instead of having fixed views for a day or a week, you simply tap and drag the days you want to see, such as Tuesday through Friday of next week. Tapping on a specific day brings up a pop-up of that day's events. You can drag and drop events, so if your client needs a home visit four days a week, which most do, you can easily add that event on multiple days in just a minute.

Plus, it's very easy to use, and much easier to navigate than almost any other calendar app out there. The cost is about $5 at the Google Play store.

Managing Your Contacts

As your senior concierge business grows, your customer list will grow as well, and you must have a way to manage that list, so you can keep track of your customers and any special needs they may have. Fortunately, there are two great apps available to just that for you.

If you have an Android phone, Contacts + is a must-have app. With over 10 million users, you know it's got to be great. What I like best is the built-in spam blocker, so you don't have to deal with spammers. In addition, Contacts+ includes a backup service for your contacts, so if you switch or lose your phone, your contacts are always available.

If you have an iPhone, my choice is called Simpler Contacts, which of course keeps things simple but still has the features to make it useful. Plus, it's very easy to learn and use. One of my favorite features allows you to send the same text message or email to a group of people.

For example, if you plan a vacation in 3 weeks, you can message or email your entire customer list to let them know. If you're having a special promotion, like a discount on new services, send it out as well. You can back up your contacts using Google Drive or Dropbox. Simpler Contacts is available at the Apple app store.

How to Get Paid on the Go

Countries around the world are moving towards alternative payments and away from cash, such as the wildly popular app, WePay, in China, which requires just a swipe of your smartphone. That's a hot trend in the U.S. and Canada as well, with cash-free services like Apple Pay and Venmo growing in popularity every day.

To handle the growing number of customers who prefer not to use cash, you'll need to provide a method for them to use a credit card easily. Fortunately, there are several companies that offer mobile payment processing for small businesses like yours. Three that stand out for affordability and ease of use are Square, SparkPay and Propay.

Square is a user-friendly payment system for accepting credit and debit cards. Square's mobile card reader, which plugs into your smart phone, is free when you sign up. Square works with both Android and Apple smartphones and tablets. They currently charge a flat 2.75% processing fee. www.square.com.

SparkPay is part of CapitalOne, the well-known credit card company, and provides a solid mobile payment system. You can start with their "Go" plan, which charges 2.65% per transaction, then switch to the "Pro" plan, when your volume hits $2,000 per month. With that volume, the fee falls to 1.99% per transaction. Users also report the customer phone support is better than Square, an important consideration. SparkPay.com.

Finally, ProPay, a service that has been around for years, offers all the features needed for mobile payment processing, including a mobile card reader, and rates as low as 2.40% for processing transactions. ProPay.com.

CHAPTER THREE

Finding Your Customers

Without new customers, your new senior concierge business will never thrive and make a profit. Marketing is an essential part of starting and growing your new business, and this chapter will give you the tools to find all the customers you want, with very little expense.

Small business owners today have far more marketing options available to them than just a few years ago. Now, because of the explosive growth of the internet as an advertising medium, many of the most effective marketing tools are free or close to it.

In additional to internet-based marketing, there are also dozens of traditional marketing methods available for any business owner that takes the time to use them. Almost all are free or almost free.

From flyers to publicity releases, smart small business owners have been using these proven methods to boost sales and profits for many years, but now, thanks to the internet, your marketing message can reach more people for less money than ever before.

I'll go over dozens of free and low-cost marketing ideas for your new business in this chapter. You don't have to use all of them – just experiment with several to see which one's work best for your business. Whether you're launching a new business or growing an existing business, free marketing can help you grow your business without spending a lot to do so.

The material we'll cover in this chapter is meant to be an idea generator for you, so skim the content, and pick the ideas that interest you. I'm sure you will find the perfect combination of ideas to boost your sales and profits for years to come.

Never forget the Golden Rule of marketing – ***treat your customers and prospects as you would want to be treated, and they will be loyal customers for life!***

Capable and dependable senior in-home concierges are hard to find. If they are good at what they do – providing high-quality services to seniors – they will always be in demand and working as much as they choose. Once you've had a few clients to give you 5-star recommendations, you can expect to be busy.

But when you are just starting out, you do not have a track record or a stellar reputation in the senior community, so you will need to advertise in order to get your first clients. Here are the 4 best ways to find clients:

Free Ads. Don't waste your money on newspaper ads – there are plenty of ways to advertise for free. Many caregivers have found a simple ad, repeated regularly on Craigslist.org can bring in a steady supply of new prospects. Here is a sample ad you can adapt for your own use:

At Your Service – Senior Concierge

Call Today for Help Today

What We Do:

Home helper service & errands

Conversation & companionship

Pickup and deliveries

Write letters & pay bills

Assist with pet care

Shop for groceries

Organize your home

Supervise home maintenance

Computer assistance

If you don't see it here – just ask!

Free Consultation – Licensed, Bonded, Insured

Your Business Name & Phone number

You should also have a simple brochure to pass out to prospects as well. Have a local graphic designer put one together for you or use an online pro from elance.com or odesk.com.

Local Referrals – 8 Best Sources

Local Referrals. Those who work with seniors regularly are the best source of referrals for your senior concierge business. Here's who to contact:

Attorneys who specialize in elder law can be an excellent source of clients, as they are often contacted when a senior has significant life changes.

Assisted Living Facilities. When seniors return home after a stay in an assisted living facility, they often need assistance with everyday tasks.

Churches. Pastors, ministers and rabbis deal regularly with the old and sick and are often aware when they need assistance at home. Leave your business card and a few brochures with each pastor you contact.

Other senior care providers. Introduce yourself to other care providers in your community to tap into this referral network.

Over 55 Communities. Almost every over 55 community publishes a monthly or quarterly newsletter for its residents. Most newsletters also allow classified ads, so check with the communities in your area, and place an ad offering your services.

Networking. Local service clubs, like Kiwanis, Rotary or the Chamber of Commerce can give your new business a big boost, especially if you have an opportunity to give a brief presentation about what you can do for seniors.

Word of mouth. Satisfied clients are the best advertisement, and far more credible than any other form of advertising. Often one happy client will recommend you to several friends, who may also become clients. Be sure to leave a few business cards with clients to pass along. Don't forget – you create satisfied clients when you provide quality service, charge fair prices and always practice the Golden Rule – ***Treat Others as You Would Want to be Treated.***

Online Referrals. Many seniors, as well as the adult children of seniors, now use the Internet to find a senior care provider. Even if you have your own website, you may want to register with the online care provider referral services. Here are a few to consider:

1. www.eldercarelink.com
2. www.actikare.com
3. Caring from a Distance. www.cfad.org
4. www.caring.com
5. www.carepathways.com
6. www.caregiver.org

Many states now maintain an online registry of home care providers. This can be a good source of referrals for your new home concierge business. To find out if your state has a registry, do a web search for "your state" home care registry.

The Best Free Advertising

Satisfied clients are a small business "secret weapon," as they are usually repeat/regular clients and they tell their friends about your business, yet your out-of-pocket advertising cost is zero. Word-of-mouth can be your most effective advertising if you provide a service that is so good your clients are loyal for years. Here are two ways to encourage your happy clients to share their enthusiasm about your business:

Always give your clients more than what they expect. Zappo's does it with free shipping and 110% customer service, bakers do it with the "baker's dozen" of an extra roll or pastry. Think about how you might surprise your clients when they choose you to help them with their needs.

Ask for word-of-mouth by asking satisfied clients to refer their friends to you. You can even "bribe" them with a discount or gift if their friend mentions their name when they buy.

Always treat your satisfied clients with loyalty, kindness and consideration (Just like you want to be treated!) The more satisfied clients you have, the more additional satisfied clients you'll gain. Like a snowball rolling downhill, it's a growing circle of boosters that gets bigger every day along with your profits.

A Smile is Still the Best Free Advertising

A simple smile is rarely mentioned in advertising textbooks or classes, but it is one of the most important marketing tools we all possess. A smile forms a powerful human bond and shows you regard a person as a human being, not just another customer or business prospect.

A smile makes a person feel good, and perhaps even feel you are a friend. As you know, folks like to buy from friends. Ask yourself how you felt the last time someone smiled at you. How did it make you feel? I thought so. Remember, smiles are free, requiring only a small amount of energy. Don't forget that a smile works when you're chatting on the phone, as the person on the other end can actually feel the smile.

Business success is all about paying attention to the little details, like a genuine smile. Share yours with every customer and prospect you meet and let it work its magic for you.

Customer Service

Marketing pros rank customer service right up there in the top three success factors for small business. In these competitive times, running a customer- focused business can make the difference between success and failure. Like most of the ideas in this chapter, customer service costs almost nothing out- of-pocket.

Frank Cooper, the author of "The Customer Signs Your Paycheck," has a checklist for business owners called:

The 10 Commandments of Customer Relations

1. The customer is never an interruption to your work. The customer is your real reason for being in business. Chores can wait.

2. Greet every customer with a friendly smile. Customers are people, and they like friendly contact. They usually return it.

3. Call customers by name. Make a game of learning customers' names. See how many you can remember. This is a valuable habit.

4. Remember–you are the company!

5. Never argue with a customer. The customer is always right (in his own eyes). Be a good listener, agree with him where you can, and then do what you can to make him happy.

6. Never say, "I don't know." If you don't know the answer to a customer's question, say, "That's a good question. Let me find out for you."

7. Remember that the customer pays your wages. Every dollar you earn comes from the customer's pocket. Treat him like the boss. He signs your paycheck.

8. State things in a positive way. Choose positive words when speaking to a customer. It takes practice, but it is a valuable habit that will help you become an effective communicator.

9. Brighten every customer's day! Make it a point to do something that brings a little sunshine into each customer's life, and soon you'll discover that your own life is happier and brighter!

10. Go the extra mile! Always do just a little more than the customer expects you to do. You will be richly rewarded for this habit!

Make Money with Reminders

Your existing customers are like money in the bank. They know you; they trust you and are far more likely to purchase from you than someone who is not yet a client. One of the easiest ways for a business to make money is to contact past customers with a special offer.

For example, send out an e-mail coupon to your client and prospect mailing list every month. The coupon could be for specials, like a 10% discount for a new customer, or a non- specific offer, like 20% off when a customer tries a new service.

Everyone loves to be remembered, so think about sending out birthday cards or personalized reminders. For some ideas, visit www.sendoutcards.com. An old-fashioned handwritten note is still an effective tool. Very few businesses take the time to do this, which makes it even more effective.

For example, drop a thank-you note in the mail to each customer two or three times a year. Nothing fancy, just let them know you appreciate them and value their business.

The simple act of communicating regularly is a powerful business builder when practiced often and sincerely. Take a few minutes every week to stay in touch with your customers, and you'll be well rewarded.

Let Google Help Your Customers Find You

If your business depends on local customers, you'll enjoy a free listing in Google Places. Today, most of your customers are using internet search engines to find local services and businesses instead of the traditional Yellow Pages. So it makes sense to take advantage of these free listings offered by online directories for businesses. The most popular, and currently the largest, of all is Google Places.

You can start by visiting http://places.google.com and clicking on the 'get started now' button under 'Get your business found on Google.' After signing in, or signing up, at no cost, you'll be able to list your business. You can include photos or add photos or a map.

Getting a basic listing is simple, but there are a few ways to help your business appear near the top of the listings if you have any local competitors listed.

First, remember Google values good content, so be sure you fill out your business profile with quality information. Follow their directions for completing the listing to the letter and don't leave any blank spaces.

Next, encourage your customers to leave feedback and positive reviews on any web sites related to your business, such as local directories published by groups like the Chamber of Commerce. You can also ask customers to leave reviews or testimonials on your own website but be sure they are legitimate and genuine.

Last, if you don't have one yet, your business needs a website, ideally with its own domain name. Having a website will give your business, however small it is, a giant boost in the Google rankings.

As more and more businesses sign up for Google Places, those who have a website will have a better shot at a listing near the top. Almost any web hosting service, such as BlueHost, mentioned earlier, can help you get a domain name and set up a Wordpress site, which ranks well with Google, as Wordpress is easy to index.

Besides Google Places, other major online 'local' directories worth exploring are:

http://bing.com/local

http://listings.local.yahoo.com

http://listings.local.yahoo.com

http://yelp.com

http://linkedin.com

http://citysearch.com

http://listings.mapquest.com

http://advertise.local.com

http://angieslist.com

Local S.E.O.

Since your new senior service business will depend on local customers, you must use location- based keywords, such as "Senior concierge business- your town." The reason local SEO is so important for your business is because almost half of all Google searches are searching for a local business.

For example, the fastest growing search term on Google is "near me" as in "Italian restaurant near me." Since Google and other search engines can easily determine your approximate location, this enables them to deliver the results you are searching for with high accuracy.

To make it even easier for you to find what you're looking for, Google provides a "Map Pack," a set of 3 high ranking local businesses, complete with a map of their locations from Google maps. Underneath the Map Pack, you'll find the rest of the results for your search.

How to find the best keywords for local S.E.O.

Do a Google search for words and phrases that relate to your business, one at a time, and make a list of them. For example, "senior concierge service near me." When you enter your search term, you'll see a list of additional search terms. Take a close look at those to see if any are suitable for your business. Save your list of search terms to use when setting up your "Google My Business" profile.

How to set up your Google My Business profile

Google My Business (www.google.com/business) is the number one factor Google uses to rank your business in local searches. When setting up your profile, be sure to include your full business name, address, and phone number (NAP). Google uses this information to ensure that your business is legitimate. Also, the NAP on your website should be an exact match for your Google My Business listing.

If it's not a match, Google may rank your business lower in local searches. Even spelling counts here – if your business address is 123 Lincoln Avenue, makes sure it's "Avenue" and not "Ave." so the Google search engine doesn't get confused.

When filling out your profile on GMB, choose a broad category that best describes your business – "senior transportation" for example. Also fill out the "services" tab in your profile that describes what your business does.

Google Reviews

Reviews are another major ranking factor in the Google ranking system. You may have noticed that business with many reviews, especially positive reviews, always ranks higher than those with no reviews. That's why you'll want to get as many positive reviews as you can as soon as you can.

When you get a review, good, bad or lukewarm, reply to it inside the Google My Business dashboard. That shows you care and is also a factor in Google rankings. It doesn't have to be a long reply to be effective. For example, "Thanks for the 5-star review. We really appreciate your business," or "Thanks for the feedback."

How to Get More Google Reviews

Keep in mind that most customers won't bother to leave a review, even if they love your service, unless asked. It's easy to do. In fact, Google makes it easy for both you and your customers.

Go to your GMB account dashboard and locate the "get more reviews" card. There, you can get a link to your review page that you can copy and paste into an email to send to your customers.

Apply all these simple SEO tips, and soon your new business will show up on page 1 of Google search results. All without having to spend any money. Don't put this off any longer than necessary, as it's one of the best "free lunches" you'll ever receive!

Social Media Marketing

Facebook is the largest social media network in the world, with over 2 billion active users. Most users are between the ages of 25 and 65, but the over-65 users are the fastest growing group! That's great news, as these are the people you want to reach about your home watch business.

Because of its size and the large number of users, Facebook is the best social media to get your new business shared and discovered by both new prospects and your current clients. That's why it is often called "the largest word-of-mouth marketing resource on the planet."

Facebook can also be the biggest time waster if you let it, as it's easy to linger there for hours. But you have a business to build and grow, so let's focus on doing just that, with some help from Facebook, in less than 15 minutes a day.

First rule – Don't waste your money on Facebook ads. No one visits Facebook to look for services or products. They visit to see what their friends are doing. With that in mind, here's how to get started without spending a dime.

It's important to note that you must create a Facebook page, not a personal profile, also called a Personal Timeline. They do not permit personal profiles for commercial use, so if you are already a Facebook user you must create a separate page for your home watch business.

You can create a Facebook Page by searching "create a page" in the searcher at the top of the page, or by clicking the "create a page" button at the top of any Facebook page.

Before you create your new Facebook page, spend some time thinking about the page name you will use. Ideally, it should be short, easy to remember, promise a benefit, and describe your business.

In the "About" section of your new Facebook Page, include as much information about your business as possible, so current clients and prospects can find all your important information in one page.

You can also optimize your page by choosing one of the pre-made templates. The Professional Services template is a good fit for most senior transportation businesses. You'll find the templates under: Settings>Edit Page.

Next, create an eye-catching cover photo for your Facebook page. Look at other senior concierge businesses on Facebook and by doing a web search for "senior concierge business" to see what others have done.

Ideally, your cover photo should communicate what your business is all about, so take the time to do it right. The easiest way to get a good cover photo designed is to hire a designer at Fiverr.com.

It will cost you around $5 to $15, but it's money well spent. Just enter "design Facebook cover" in the Fiverr.com search bar to locate dozens of capable designers. Be sure to mention that you want the image size to be 820 X 312 pixels per Facebook guidelines.

When you've uploaded your new cover photo, click it to add a text description. Describe your business in a positive way and, if possible, encourage viewers to click on the cover photo to get more "likes."

You'll also want to add a Facebook profile photo in a 180 x 180-pixel size. Remember, this profile photo appears in a follower's news feeds, in comment replies, and all over Facebook, so use a great photo. (Don't forget to smile!)

Once you've set up your Facebook page, stay active with regular posts. Most pros find 3X a week works well yet doesn't require a lot of time.

Don't forget to post about special experiences you've had with clients that others might enjoy. Share the story and a picture or two of you and your client in a post.

Is a Facebook Page Better Than a Web Site?

Yes, and no. You can set up a Facebook page in about an hour and it's free. That page allows you to stay in touch with clients and prospects and build relationships. If a Facebook page is not working for you delete it or ignore it. Keeping your Facebook page up to date with your current information, such as rates and services offered, is quick and easy.

But – you are not in control. Facebook is in control and can change or restrict what you can do on the site overnight. In addition, anyone can post negative comments or complaints on your page if they wish.

If you create a website, you're in control. You own it. You get to decide what it looks like and what it contains. You can have hundreds of pages or posts or just a simple one-pager.

Consumers today expect a business to have a website. They trust a business more when they see a "real" website. Also, having your own website allows you to post all your service information at the site, like the services you provide, monthly specials, testimonials and more.

My choice would be to have both a Facebook page and a website. You have the best of both worlds – and you don't have to say "follow me on Facebook."

Twitter can be a powerful social media tool for your business that can help you educate clients about your services, reach new prospects for your business and connect you to other Twitter users with similar interests.

Here are just two of the many ways Twitter can help your business:

- ✓ Drive traffic to your website. Unlike other social media, you can re-use content from your website or other original material repeatedly. Your tweets can include your website URL, text, images, even a video.

- ✓ Google indexes your twitter bio and tweets, which helps you get found by search engines. Make sure your bio contains the keywords you want Google to find and index, such as your business name and what your business does. Be sure to tweet regularly so you increase the odds of ranking higher in Google Search.

Last, use hashtags (#) to get more attention for your tweets, show your support and help people who don't know you to follow you. To learn what topics are hot or trending up right now, check Twitter Trends or hashtagify.me.

It's free and easy to make an account – just visit twitter.com, enter your name, phone and email address and create a password for your new account. After you've signed up, you can add more information for your account.

Next it's time to pick your Twitter "handle," which is the same as a username. The best handle is your business name, if it is available. You can check all the social networks for name availability at knowem.com.

If your handle/name is not available, you can add HQ to your company name, add a "get" in front of your name, or add your location, such as your town's name, to your handle.

Whatever handle you choose, make sure it is as short as possible, because you only have 280 characters to use, and they count your username in that 280 words when someone responds to your messages.

LinkedIn is a place for companies and individuals to connect on a professional, not personal, level. Unlike other social media sites, folks who join LinkedIn are not joining for enjoyment and fun but to access new business opportunities and connections.

As the owner of a small business, you can use LinkedIn to connect to other related service businesses, promote your own business and build relationships with other professionals that have common interests.

Getting started is no more difficult than at other social networks. You start by creating your own personal account and profile. A LinkedIn profile is much more professional You won't find funny cat videos or cute baby photos.

Keep that in mind when creating your profile. In your profile, be sure to include your best work-related qualities so others will see the advantages of working with you.

Although you can upgrade to several higher levels of paid subscriptions, the basic account should be fine for almost all small businesses. Your basic profile can include a summary of yourself, contact information, links to your blog or website or other social media pages, like Facebook, and what you're doing now professionally.

Once you've completed your personal profile and published it, you can:

- Look for connections – people you know or would like to know.
- Join a group of other users who share common interests.
- Have an online "business card" where potential clients can learn about and connect with you.
- Boost your online reputation as a senior services professional.

There are hundreds of other social media sites, as you may have noticed when you visited knowem.com. but most are useful only for entertainment, not helping you grow your house watch business. These three, Facebook, Twitter and LinkedIn will help you stay connected, expand your network, and increase your profits.

Stay in Touch with a Free Newsletter

One of the best and least expensive ways to stay in touch with your clients and potential clients is by sending them an e-mail newsletter. By using an email, the big expenses of a traditional newsletter, printing and postage, are eliminated. Your newsletter should do two things:

- Pass along useful information your customers are happy to read, even forward to their friends.

- Increase your profits by either helping sell more of your services or attract more prospects who will buy from you.

The easiest way to make sure your newsletter accomplishes those two goals is to just ask your clients and prospects what they want before you send out the first issue and keep asking them what they want in the newsletter. How often should a newsletter be sent to clients? Most experts say it's not how often that matters, but the quality of the content.

Some prefer a frequent schedule, such as every two weeks or once a month, while others may only do a quarterly newsletter. If you have built a list of loyal clients, they don't really care how often they receive an issue.

Be sure to ask a favor at the end of each newsletter: "If you've enjoyed this newsletter, please forward it to your friends." Doing so will grow your subscriber list and your profits over time.

When your e-mail list has grown beyond a few subscribers, it's time to get some professional help. My favorites are www.MailChimp.com and www.mailerlite.com

At Mail Chimp, for free, you'll have access to professionally designed message templates and sign-up forms, and up to 2,000 customers or 12,000 emails a month and compliance with all anti-spam regulations.

You'll love the free service, plus the freedom from tedious mailing list maintenance. Another excellent provider with free service for up to 1,000 subscribers is mailerlite.com.

Ten Tips for a Successful E-Mail Newsletter

According to the e-mail pros, a well-done e-mail newsletter can produce $40 in profits for every dollar you spend. That's a powerful incentive to spend the time on staying in touch with your customers and prospects with e-mails. Here are ten tips that will help you make more money and build customer loyalty with your own e-mail newsletter:

- Current content. Be sure to date each newsletter issue when you send it out so readers will know the content is current.

- You don't have to be a writer to produce an e-mail newsletter that gets results. Just write as you speak and focus on the topic you want to communicate with your clients.

- Your newsletter need not look professional to succeed. Just a simple text message will work just fine. That said, most of the professional e-mail list management services, like www.MailerLite.com.com and www.MailChimp.com offer free HTML templates that can dress up your message.

- The best ideas for content in your e-mail newsletter will come from your readers. Ask them often about what they would like to see covered in future issues.

- Keep your newsletter short. If you have several ideas to share, break them up into individual newsletter issues, or include an excerpt, with a link to the full text at your web site or blog.

- Try not to go too long between issues – two weeks to a month is a reasonable interval to aim for.

- The cyber-gremlins will always try to mess with your e-mails, so get used to it. E-mails get lost, trapped in reader's spam filters, or just plain disappear. Subscribers will forget they subscribed and accuse you of spamming them or click the spam button instead of unsubscribing. Just view it all as a part of your learning curve and stay calm. Using one of the services mentioned in #3 can help minimize problems, and the cost is reasonable. In fact, as I write this, Mail Chimp and MailerLite offer a free service if you have a small (1,000 to 2,000 subscribers) list.

- Keep your sales pitches under control. While folks expect you to sell them something, they get upset if it occurs with every newsletter issue. Experts say a ratio of 80 percent informational content to 20 percent sales information is about right.

- Stay on topic. Your readers gave you their e-mail address so they could learn more about topics related to protecting their valuable home while they're away and other related topics. Stay away from personal topics, as some will enjoy learning about your personal life, but an equal amount will not care, and be inclined to hit the spam button or unsubscribe.

- Also, post your newsletters on your website or blog so readers can find them at a later date. In addition, the search engines will spot and index them, and help steer new prospects to your site.

Your Own Senior Concierge Website

A simple website is the best way to advertise your senior concierge business. A website is the new 21st century version of traditional Yellow Pages advertising, because most prospects expect to find your business, or any other services and products, on the Internet.

If you think putting up a website is expensive, think again. The cost of hosting a website has dropped over the last few years, so today you can get high quality hosting for under $10 a month, with all the bells and whistles that used to be expensive are now included for free with hosting.

Three Reasons Your New Senior Concierge Business Needs a Website

Today, a website is an essential marketing tool for any business, and even more so for a senior service business. Whether you provide in-home senior care, senior transportation, senior concierge services, or senior relocation services, a simple website can help you find new customers and stay in touch with existing clients.

A website can help you build your senior service business in 3 ways:

- Market your senior service to new prospects.
- Educate consumers about your services.
- Help prospects and current customers contact you.

If you're new to building a website, make a list of what you want to accomplish before building your site. For example, do you want to make it easy for new prospects to learn more about your services before they contact you? How about a page that contains a sample service agreement that customers or prospects can read or print?

Most basic senior service websites include a FAQ page that contains all the frequently asked questions and answers about your senior services, a contact page with both phone and email contact information, a page listing the services you offer, and, after you have them, testimonials from satisfied customers. It can be helpful to visit other senior service websites to see what others are doing as well.

If you are like most new business startups, your advertising/ marketing budget is tiny. Why not harness the power of the Internet to build your business, without spendings a lot of money, by signing up for website hosting with one of the companies that offers not only affordable hosting services, but also free help to create your website?

You may have heard about hosting companies that offer free hosting, but here's why you should only consider paid hosting for your senior service website:

- You can use, and control, your own personal or business domain name, such as "Monroeseniorconcierge.com". When you have registered your domain name, you own the name, which can help your search engine visibility when prospects search for a senior concierge business.

- Paid web hosting is very affordable, and you will get better tools and resources to help you create and maintain your website.

- More design options. Using paid hosting will allow you to choose the best design, or "theme," for your site, instead of the limited choices from free hosting services.

- No ads. Free hosting companies may place ads on your website. That's how they make money, even though your website hosting is technically "free."

I'm a big fan of WordPress to build a website. Although it started as a blogging program, WordPress has now become a capable, yet user-friendly site builder that can be customized to meet the needs of almost any senior service business.

With thousands of free themes and free help from a huge online forum of users, it may be the best way to build an affordable website. In addition, there are thousands of "widgets" and "plugins" that can be added to your website to provide additional features like videos, shopping carts or customer surveys.

Even if you're not a tech-savvy person, setting up, maintaining and adding to your site is easy enough for most users to do themselves. If you do need help, sites like elance.com and odesk. com can provide affordable, knowledgeable pros to help.

I use Bluehost for my website hosting, because it's so easy to use, with a free domain name, 1-click automatic WordPress installation, free email accounts, and great customer service by phone, chat or email 24/7. I highly recommend Bluehost for your first website. I make this recommendation only because I personally have used Bluehost hosting for many years and found their service to be exceptional.

Sample Senior Concierge Website

A basic website for your senior concierge business should contain five essential pages to start, then you can add more as needed. You may adapt the information listed below to use for your own website.

Home Page/Welcome Page

The home page of your website is the first page a visitor will see. Use the welcome page to provide a brief overview of your business. Here is a sample of text you could use for your welcome page:

Welcome ...

"Your Company Name"

*Affordable, Compassionate Help for Seniors.
You can trust us for senior concierge and
companionship services.*

Thanks to improved medical care, more seniors are living well into their 80s and 90s. Many are capable of maintaining their independence at home with some outside help and assistance. That's what we do.

We help seniors stay in their own home and enjoy an independent life. At home, surrounded by familiar things, seniors experience less stress and live happier, healthier, longer lives.

Our Simple Mission ... Our caring and capable concierge service for seniors help our clients live a safe and independent life in their own home. We provide peace of mind – at no extra charge!

To learn more about what we can offers, click on "our services" in the menu bar above.

About Us Page

Your Company Name was founded by *Your Name* (put your photo here.) to provide high-quality concierge services to seniors in *Your Town.* – seniors living alone who are at great risk for falls, medication errors and mental stress from loneliness and isolation.

We Respect Your Privacy ... We help seniors stay safe and happy in their own home – at affordable prices. All information about our clients and their families is kept strictly confidential.

We are Licensed, Bonded and Insured to protect our clients. Our rates are reasonable and affordably priced at only .... per hour. Our rates reflect high-quality service.

Shopping for the lowest price may be okay for groceries, but not the services of a trained senior concierge. Remember ... Hiring a "bargain" concierge can be a risky decision that far outweighs the money you might save.

We are active, semi-retired people who love helping others! Mature senior helpers are more in touch with the needs and desires of seniors. They are patient and positive, with great people skills. In addition, they are dependable, honest and caring. For you, this translates into peace of mind, and the highest quality of service.

Our Senior Concierge Services

Your Company Name provides affordable solutions to seniors who need assistance with their daily activities. We can help you and your loved ones with a wide variety of services, such as:

✓ Errands and grocery shopping.

✓ Home safety checks.

✓ Light housekeeping.

✓ Meal preparation and menu planning

✓ Medication reminders.

✓ Transportation to appointments.

✓ Write letters and correspondence

✓ Organize closets, cabinets & garages

✓ Assist with pet care

✓ Accompany to lunch, dinner or events

✓ Trip planning & reservations

✓ Supervise home maintenance

✓ Monitor diet & exercise

✓ Set up automatic bill paying or assist with submitting payments

✓ Monitor bank statements & insurance bills & payments

These personalized services are available 7 days a week and can be customized to meet individual needs.

Our services are a perfect solution for seniors who want to remain independent as long as possible. Give us a call today to discuss your needs and questions. (*Your phone number here*)

Contact Us Page

Simply list your contact information on this page or use something more formal. I use a free WordPress plugin called the "Fast Secure Contact Form," which, just as the name says, prevents spammers from sending junk mail to your email inbox.

Resources Page

Frequently Asked Questions

How is your senior concierge service different from senior home care services? Senior home care services are more focused on health care. A concierge service provides other personal services, such as errand running, personal assistance, personal bookkeeping and companionship, all through one personal concierge.

Do you have references? Yes, we can provide references, as well as proof of bonding, insurance and licensing, on request. Please visit our "About Us" page to learn more about the owner.

How do I know you will be available when needed? We work with a limited number of clients at a time, to ensure that we will have ample time to devote to each of our senior clients.

How do I pay for your services? We provide an itemized invoice at the end of each month, or project. This is sent to either the senior we are helping, or a designated family member. You can pay by check or credit card.

Alzheimer's

The National Alzheimer's Association has several helpful free guides to coping with Alzheimer's disease, ranging from the basics to caregiving to safety, treatments and "Know the 10 signs of Alzheimer's." (www.alz.org/alzheimers_disease_publications.asp)

The Alzheimer's Foundation of America provides a wide range of publications about Alzheimer's, as well as a free hot line (866-232-8484) for caregivers, staffed by social workers. www.alzfdn.org

Elder Abuse

The National Center on Elder Abuse (www.ncea.aoa.gov) offers a variety of helpful resources to educate the public and assist victims of elder abuse, including links to local hotlines and prevention programs.

Fall Prevention

The U.S. Consumer Products Safety Commission (www.cpsc.gov) has put together a free booklet on *"Safety for Older Consumers – Home Safety Checklist."* That covers all the essentials needed to prevent falls and accidents in and around the home.

Fraud & Identity Theft

When it comes to elder fraud, why not learn from the top dog – the FBI. At their senior citizen fraud page, you'll find a comprehensive list of the most common frauds and scams, from telemarketing fraud, identity theft, advance fee schemes, investment scams, internet fraud, reverse mortgage fraud, even counterfeit prescription drugs, and how to protect yourself or your loved ones. www.fbi.gov/scams-safety/fraud/seniors

---

What to Do When a Prospect Calls You

Prospect inquiries are the fuel for your senior concierge business because they turn into paying clients to help grow your business income. Most of your inquiries will be phone calls from prospects who spotted your ad on Craigslist, found your website, or heard about you from a happy client or other senior care professional.

It's important to make yourself available, so use a cell phone number in your ads, or forward your landline/voicemail to your cell phone when you will be away from the office.

If your phone has caller ID, and you don't recognize the name, introduce yourself professionally. For example: *"This is Nicole, with Magnolia Senior Concierge Service ... May I help you?"* Once you have determined the caller is a prospect for your service, try to get their contact information: *"May I have your name and number in case we get disconnected?"*

Keep the New Prospect Form handy, so you can use it to get all the information you'll need to decide if you can help the prospect, and the rate you will quote them. After you have filled out the form, pre-qualify the prospect: *"Is this rate within your budget?"* You'll often find that folks have no idea what the cost of a concierge service is, and simply can't afford it, or afford as many hours as are needed.

Often a prospect will let you know that other providers have lower rates. Here's what to tell them: *"With senior concierge services, lower rates can mean lower quality. A lower priced provider may not have insurance or be bonded. You do want the best care for your mom ... Right?"*

If a prospect is still interested, set up an appointment to discuss their needs and options. In the *Senior Concierge Forms* chapter, we'll cover the forms you will need at this appointment.

Follow Up With Prospects

Prospects need a reminder that builds on your conversation during the interview. For example, a phone conversation might go like this:

> *"It was good speaking with you last Friday, Mr. Smith. I could tell you were looking for the best possible assistance for your mom. That's our specialty – high quality service that helps our clients live an independent life. Thanks for making time in your schedule to learn about our services. If I can help in the future, don't hesitate to call me."*

You can convey the same message with a postcard or a letter, but don't send an email, as many people feel it is too impersonal. A simple follow-up is a time-tested, proven, technique for winning new clients, and the cost is next to nothing.

CHAPTER FOUR

Understanding Seniors

We all grow old, and as we do, we experience changes to our bodies and minds that affect our abilities, behavior and personality. The speed at which we age varies greatly from person to person, as does our ability to handle aging.

Biological loss is the aging of our physical body, which is caused or influenced by a variety of factors, such as heredity (the genes we inherit from a parent), wear and tear, weakened immune system, and a variety of chemical and structural changes in the body.

Functional Loss As we age, we experience functional loss, which can make us more dependent on others. Functional loss includes:

- ✓ Falls and other injuries.
- ✓ Hearing loss.
- ✓ Illness, such as cancer or diabetes.
- ✓ Loss of mobility.
- ✓ Osteoporosis – brittle or weakened bones.
- ✓ Vision issues, such as glaucoma.

You can help seniors deal with functional decline by encouraging them to do some form of exercise every day. This can be as simple as walking, stretching or lifting weights. Always have your client's doctor review exercise plans before starting any exercise program.

Another way you can assist is to help your client prevent falls. Falls can lead to a downhill slide in a senior's overall health, especially if the fall causes a broken limb or hip. Start with our senior home safety checklist in chapter 7.

Social Isolation Seniors need social interaction, but as they age, it can become more difficult to meet and socialize with others. This can be caused by a loss of mobility, a chronic illness, or the loss of a spouse or loved one. Social isolation often leads to substance abuse, such as excess alcohol consumption, poor eating habits that can cause nutritional issues, and increased anxiety or depression.

You can help clients who are isolated by encouraging more social activities, community events and activities, like a visit to the local senior center for lunch. Self-esteem plays a big role here, so be positive to help your client feel needed and valued. If they are no longer able to drive, look into the local dial-a-ride service, a friend with a vehicle or even by driving them yourself.

Substance Abuse Excess use of alcohol or drugs can affect coordination, reaction time and balance, and make seniors more prone to falls or other injuries. Also, as we age, our bodies process both alcohol and medications differently than when we were younger, so what have might have been okay at fifty could be fatal at seventy-five.

Causes of senior substance abuse include health issues, financial issues, moving, retirement, death of a spouse or friend and loneliness. A senior may also drink or abuse prescription drugs to calm nerves, numb pain or reduce depression.

Be alert to the possibility of substance abuse, especially if a client is mixing alcohol with prescription drugs that could interact with alcohol. If you see signs of a problem, contact the client's primary care doctor, or another health care professional who may be able to help your client.

How to Communicate with Your Senior Clients

Communicating with seniors can often be challenging, as the elderly may have physical or mental issues that require more patience and compassion. But is essential to learn the basic communication skills so you can understand and help your clients. Here are six essential tips to focus on:

- Use open-ended questions that require more than just a yes or no answer. You will learn more from your clients if you take this approach.

- Sit face-to-face, which gives your clients the feeling you think they are important. Many older people have hearing loss and rely on lip-reading to understand what you are saying.

- Pay attention to make sure your client understands what you are saying. If they don't seem to understand, rephrase it instead of repeating it. Do not speak louder.

- Maintain eye contact to pick up non-verbal hints, and touch when appropriate.

- Show interest in what your client is saying, even if you've heard it many times before.

- Instead of telling your clients what to do, show them.

Listening

- Listening can be just as important as speaking when communicating with clients. Try these techniques with your clients:

- Be respectful of your client, and non-judgmental.

- Try to be aware of when to stop listening and start talking.

- Listen without speaking when dealing with angry or upset clients.

- Maintain eye contact, and avoid distractions, like your cell phone.

- If you don't understand what they are saying, ask for clarification.

- Don't cross your arms – it sends the message that you have already made up your mind.

Are you guilty of "Elderspeak?"

Many of us, often without even realizing they are doing it, use "Elderspeak," or baby talk aimed at seniors. It implies that the senior is incompetent, frail, dependent or child-like, and that all seniors suffer from memory or hearing problems.

Here's how to spot Elderspeak:

- ✓ Speaking slower or louder than normal.
- ✓ Using a sing-song voice.
- ✓ Using "we" and "our" in place of "you." For example, "How are we doing today?"
- ✓ Using cute names like "honey," "dearie," or "sweetheart."
- ✓ Answering questions instead of asking them. "You would like your lunch now, wouldn't you?"
- ✓ Shortening or simplifying sentences.

Eldercare experts have found that when seniors are exposed to Elderspeak, they feel that people are talking down to them, which can cause them to get angry, refuse to cooperate, even cause depression.

Using Elderspeak with your clients can trigger feelings of incompetence, decreased self-esteem, withdrawal or anger. To avoid Elderspeak, begin a conversation by asking the client what they would like to be called, and respect their age and elder status. Pay attention to the way they react to your language. Avoid terms of endearment, such as "sweetie" or "honey."

A recent study by Dr. Becca Levy found that seniors who had a positive attitude about aging lived an average of 7 years longer – a larger increase than for exercising regularly or not smoking! You can help them retain that positive attitude by avoiding Elderspeak and boosting their self-esteem whenever possible.

If you want to help your senior clients live a longer and happier life, watch your words, as they can be very powerful in both positive and negative ways, and never call one "sweetie."

Difficult Clients

Most senior clients are grateful for your assistance, and easy to be around. Unfortunately, you will encounter the occasional difficult client, and must deal with them in a way that enables you to do your job effectively. Here are a few tips for handling difficult clients:

- Don't take it personally. Your client's behavior is a reflection on where they are at in life. Being elderly or sick or frail can be scary, and that can affect how they interact with you.

- Set boundaries. When necessary, teach your clients how to treat you today and in the future. For example: "I treat you respectfully, and I expect the same in return."

- Acknowledge their feelings. You don't have to agree, but just let them vent their feelings. This will help them feel valued and appreciated.

- Hold your ground. Difficult clients are often in love with their misery and suffering and will dial it up a notch or two if you give in to them.

CHAPTER FIVE

Senior Concierge Forms

In the pages that follow, you'll find the essential forms for your new senior concierge service. As a purchaser of this guidebook, you also may copy, adapt and use these forms for your own concierge service only.

These forms have not been reviewed by an attorney and are meant as a guide only. We encourage you to have an attorney review the forms to ensure they are appropriate for your specific needs and the laws and regulations that apply in your state and city or town before you use them.

New prospect form. Keep several of these forms near your phone so you can get enough information written down when a prospect calls to decide: Is this someone I can help? Do I have the necessary skills to do a good job for this client?

After you have had a chance to chat with the new prospect, suggest a meeting to go over the client's needs and what you can do for them. The first meeting will usually take between one-half to one hour. Your goal is to establish trust and confidence and bring up any special skills or experience you have that would make you a good fit with the client.

Begin the meeting by discussing areas where the client needs assistance, such as transportation or meal preparation. If the client or a family member agree, check that box, then review the next item, until you have reviewed all the service possibilities. Be sure to ask if there are other areas they would like to discuss.

Don't forget, at this first meeting, that you are an unknown to your potential client, so smile and be positive about what you can do to help and be patient and understanding with them.

Bring a service agreement and a client information form to the first meeting. If things go well, you can get both forms completed and have the client or a family member sign the service agreement.

Service agreement. This agreement spells out the working relationship between you and your client, which may be the person you will be helping, or a "responsible person," such as a son, daughter or guardian. To help prevent misunderstandings, this agreement spells out the services you will be providing, the hourly rate, any surcharges, mileage charges and your cancellation policy.

Client information form. This information should be filled out with the help of the senior you will be helping, or the person who is responsible for their care. It covers emergency contacts, physician contact information, any known allergies or diet restrictions, and a brief summary of the client's medical condition.

Key release form. The key release form is used if you need a key to access your client's home for tasks such as pet sitting or to deliver groceries or other purchases when the client is not at home.

Grocery delivery order form. The grocery delivery order form makes it very easy for your client to spell out in detail what they want and when they want it. Leave extra order forms with your regular customers and be sure to put your phone number on all forms to make it easy for a client to reach you.

Pet sitting agreement. This agreement will help you remember all the small details about a client's pet, from names to special instructions for feeding and medications. Many seniors worry more about their pets than themselves, so this form will give them confidence in your ability to take care of every last detail.

Errand log sheet. Carry these forms with you at all times, so when you are running errands, you can accurately track mileages, costs and time.

New Prospect Form

Date _____

Client Name _____

_____

Phone _____

Caller Name _____

Phone _____

Relationship to client: _____

_____

Decision maker: _____

_____

Services Needed:

- Companionship
- Meal preparation
- Errands & transportation
- Household management
- Grocery shopping
- Bill paying

- Light housekeeping
- Home organization
- Pet services

Is client ambulatory? _____

Devices Used:

- Cane or walker
- Scooter
- Commode
- Wheelchair

Interview appointment date: _____

Time: _____

With: _____

Address: _____

_____

Service Agreement

This agreement is entered into between _____

_____, hereinafter called "Service Provider"

and_____

____, hereinafter called "client."

Client's address: _____

_____

Client's phone number: _____

 Client's email address: _____

The service provider agrees to provide the following services to:

_____

_____ Client,

At: _____

_____address.

- ☐ Bill paying
- ☐ Light housekeeping
- ☐ Pet services
- ☐ Errands and transportation

☐ Home organizing

☐ Caring companionship

☐ Meal preparation

☐ Grocery shopping

☐ Household management

☐ Other: _____

Client is aware that service provider provides concierge services only and is not licensed to provide medical care.

Client agrees to pay service provider at an hourly rate of $_____

Weekend hours are an additional $_____ per hour. National holiday hours are time and one-half the regular rate. The rate is based on caring for one person.

Use of care provider's vehicle for incidental transportation will be billed at: _____ per mile when the caregiver is driving at the request of client, but not for commuting to and from work.

Service provider will bill client weekly. Client agrees to pay service provider on receipt of the invoice.

Client agrees to provide at least one-week advance cancellation notice. If client does not provide notice, they will be invoiced and responsible for the normally scheduled visits.

Service provider may cancel without notice for non-payment, or if they feel the care provider is at risk.

Client's signature: _____

Date: _____

Service provider's signature: _____

Client Information Form

Name, address & phone number: _____

_____

_____

_____

_____

_____

Today's date: _____

Start date: _____

Client age: _____

Primary care physician and phone number: _____

_____

_____

Emergency contact #1: _____

_____

Home phone: _____

Cell phone: _____

Emergency contact #1: _____

_____

Home phone: _____

Cell phone: _____

Diet Restrictions: _____

_____

_____

_____

_____

Food Allergies: _____

_____

_____

Medical Conditions/Diagnosis: _____

_____

_____

_____

_____

Medications: _____

_____

_____

_____

Personal Information

Other In-home caregivers?

Name: _____

_____

Phone: _____

Children? _____

Visitation Frequency? _____

Pets? _____

Care required? _____ Veterinarian? _____

_____

Vet's phone? _____

Able to drive? _____

Special needs? _____

Key Release Form

Customer _____ agrees to give

_____

a key to their home located at: _____

_____

_____ will safeguard
customer's keys, including tagging and coding keys so,
in case of loss or theft of keys, no personal information
is shown on keys.

Please choose one of the following return options:

I would like you to keep my keys for future services.

Initial here: _____

I would like you to return my keys no later than ____ days
after my return home.

Initial here: _____

I would like you to leave my keys with the authorized
person listed below.

Initial here: _____

Name: _____

Phone: _____

Address: _____

_____

Important: We will not leave your house key unattended in your home for security reasons. Because of the possibility of return delays or accidents, your home or pet could be exposed to risk. For your safety and security, we will only return your keys to you or the person you've authorized. We are not liable for any loss or damage to home if others also have access to your home.

Key Pickup:

Customer: _____

Date: _____

Key Return:

Customer: _____

Date: _____

Grocery Delivery Order Form

Customer: _____

_____

Phone: _____

Delivery Address: _____

_____

Requested Delivery Date & Time: _____

_____

Grocery List

ITEM	QUANTITY	SIZE	BRAND	COMMENTS

Pet Sitting Service Agreement

CONTACT INFORMATION

Name: _____

_____

Home Address: _____

_____

Home Phone: _____

Business Phone: _____

Cell Phone: _____

Email Address: _____

Date & Time Leaving: _____

_____

Date & Time Returning: _____

_____

PET INFORMATION

Pet's Names: _____

_____

Breed & Ages: _____

_____

Feeding Instructions: _____

_____

Medication Instructions: _____

_____

Favorite Toys & Treats: _____

_____

Number of Visits per Day: _____

Special Requests: _____

_____

Veterinarian Preference: _____

_____

Vet's Phone: _____

Are Pets Secure in Home or Yard? _____

TERMS AND CONDITIONS

The parties agree as follows: The initial term of this agreement shall be from_____
through _____

The fee is _____ per visit x (number of visits): Total: _____

The fee for each additional pet per visit is: _____
_____ Total: _____

Pet sitter is authorized to provide care and services as outlined in this contract. Pet sitter is also authorized by customer to seek emergency veterinary care if necessary, with release from all liability. If the specified veterinarian is unavailable, pet sitter is authorized to seek medical/emergency treatment as recommended by another veterinarian. Customer agrees to reimburse pet sitter for expenses incurred, plus any additional fees for sitter's time.

In the event of inclement weather or natural disaster, pet sitter is entrusted to use their best judgment in caring for pet(s) and customer's home. Pet sitter will be held harmless for consequences related to such decisions.

Pet sitter agrees to provide the services stated in this agreement in a reliable, caring and trustworthy manner. In consideration of those services, and as a condition thereof, the customer waives and relinquishes any and all claims against said pet sitter except those arising from negligence or willful misconduct on the part of the pet sitter.

Due to the unpredictability of animals, pet sitter cannot accept responsibility for any mishaps of any extraordinary or unusual nature (biting, furniture damage, accidental death, etc.) or any complications related to providing medication for pets. Nor is the pet sitter liable for injury, disappearance, death or fines of pet(s) with outdoor access.

Customer is responsible for prompt payment of fees upon completion of services contracted. A finance charge of _____% per month will be added to unpaid balances after ten days. A handling fee of _____ will be charged on all returned checks. A 50 percent deposit is required for first time customers and lengthy assignments over 14 days. In the event it is necessary to initiate collection proceedings on the unpaid charges, customer will be responsible for all attorney's fees and costs of collection.

In the event of personal emergency or illness of pet sitter, customer authorizes pet sitter to arrange for another qualified person to fulfill the duties itemized in this agreement. Client will be notified if this is necessary.

All pets must have current vaccinations. If pet sitter is bitten or otherwise exposed to any disease received from customer's pet(s), it will be the customer's responsibility to pay all costs and damages incurred by the victim.

Pet sitter reserves the right to terminate this contract at any time. If pet sitter, in their sole discretion, determines that customer's pet poses a danger to the health or safety of the pet sitter, customer authorizes pet to be placed in a kennel, with all charges to be charged and paid by customer.

I have reviewed this Service Agreement and understand and agree to all the terms and conditions.

Date: _____

Customer: _____

_____

Pet Sitter: _____

_____

Errand Log

Today's date: _____

Client name: _____

_____

Pickup from: _____

_____

Deliver to: _____

_____

Mileage:

Start: _____

Finish: _____

Total Time: _____

Paid by: ( )Cash ( )Credit card ( )Check

Reimbursed by client? _____

Receipt to client? _____

Notes:_____

_____

Today's date: _____

Client name: _____

_____

Pickup from: _____

_____

Deliver to: _____

_____

Mileage:

Start: _____

Finish:_____

Total Time: _____

Paid by: ( )Cash ( )Credit card ( )Check

Reimbursed by client? _____

Receipt to client? _____

Notes:_____

_____

_____

CHAPTER SIX

Working with
Service Vendors

A senior concierge wears many hats – errand runner, home organizer, grocery shopper – but no one expects you to do it all. A good concierge knows when to call outside help from service vendors like plumbers, painters and pet sitters in order to keep clients smiling and keep the personal workload manageable.

One of the most important tasks for you when starting a senior concierge service is to find and meet outside service providers that can help your clients when the need arises. For example, a client's old furnace is getting crankier every day. Do you have a trusted service provider you can call for help?

If you handle this aspect of your concierge business well, you will have happy clients who are pleased that a project was well done, at an affordable price. The service vendor you recommended is happy, because he or she got a profitable job from your referral. And you should be happy as well, if you pre-arranged a modest ten percent commission or referral fee in advance from your preferred service providers.

How to Find Reliable Vendors

To find qualified service vendors, ask your friends and family whom they have used in the past, with good results. Another proven and widely used method is to sign up for Angie's List online (Angieslist.com), where you can find detailed reviews on handymen, house cleaners, painters, plumbers, remodelers, tree trimmers, and dozens more skilled trades people. Each contractor is ranked from A to F for quality, price, punctuality and professionalism, and reviews from real customers are posted on the web site.

Ideally, you should have a list of pre-screened service vendors ready to go for your clients, with one preferred vendor in each of the following categories:

- Accountant/bookkeeper
- Furnace/air conditioning contractor
- Window blind & shades
- Builder/remodeler
- Carpet cleaner
- Computer specialist
- House cleaner
- Electrician

- Handyman
- Florist
- Landscaper

Financial or investment advisors, lawyers and realtors are not on this list, as they can't legally pay a commission or referral fee. You should still have a preferred provider in each area, as your clients will benefit if you can refer them to a trustworthy person in each category. You'll also find most financial advisors, lawyers and realtors are happy to send a prospect your way as well.

How to Collect Commissions from Vendors

There are quite a few ways to make this work smoothly for you. Many concierges prefer to work directly with a vendor, then submit their own bill for the service to their client and deduct the commission when they pay the vendor. This method can often lead to cash flow problems if your client does not pay promptly and opens up legal issues as well.

For example, if you get paid for a remodeling job directly from a client, then get paid by the companies who actually did the work, such as a builder, a plumber and an electrician, some states would consider you to be acting as a general contractor.

The simplest method is to send any vendors a bill for the 10% commission at the end of the month after the work was completed. For example, if a plumber did a project costing $800 at your client's home in July, send him a bill for the $80 commission due at the end of July. This method protects you from being stuck in the middle if there are any issues between your client and the vendor.

Here is a sample letter you can use to sign up service vendors:

> Your name, address & phone number
>
> Date:
>
> Dear (Vendor's name)
>
> We would like to invite you to become a preferred vendor on our senior concierge referral list. Here's how our referral service works:

We offer concierge services to many seniors in our area, who prefer to have help with many of these projects due to their age or the specialized nature of the work, such as furnace maintenance and repair. Most of these tasks, like plumbing, electrical, or yard maintenance, are service we outsource to qualified service providers who can provide the highest level of quality work.

We understand that you also have the same high standards for customer service and satisfaction that we do and invite you to become part of our team as a service vendor.

This is an informal arrangement, with no contracts to sign or forms to fill out. All we ask is a reasonable 10% commission for every referral we send you that results in a sale for you.

As part of our client service, we follow up to ensure they are satisfied with the work. At that point, we send you an invoice for the amount of the commission. If you would like to participate in our preferred provider program, just sign and date below, and return this letter to us.

Signature _____ Date: _____

If you have any questions, please call us at: _____

We look forward to working with you to help our senior clients enjoy their lives to the fullest.

Best regards,

*   *   *

Safeguard Visits – the ideal "add-on" service for your senior concierge business.

For every senior that requires regular visits, there are many more who could use a "safeguard" visit at least once or twice a week. These seniors are usually living independently at home, and for the most part, able to take care of their day-to-day needs without daily help.

Seniors living alone risk falls and other accidents, mental stress due to isolation, loneliness, and medication errors. Many do not have family living nearby, such as adult children, who could visit their parents regularly. Many adult children live too far away to visit and need a "surrogate" son or daughter to visit their elderly parent or parents.

This is where you can help. By offering regular safeguard visits, you can ensure the senior's home is checked for fall safety, (you'll find a checklist in the resources chapter) and that they are doing well.

After each visit, you can call or email the relative who requested the safeguard visits to let them know that their parent is safe and secure. This simple, yet powerful service can bring so much peace of mind for those who are unable to visit regularly.

A safeguard visit lasts about a half-hour, and you follow a simple checklist that includes the following areas, plus any items that a relative may ask you to check:

- ✓ Personal safety check. Take a quick look around to see if there is anything that could cause a fall or other accident.
- ✓ Observe appearance and demeanor – any changes from the last visit?
- ✓ Make sure your client is taking their medications as required.
- ✓ Check room temperature and adjust thermostat if necessary.
- ✓ Companionship. Sit down with your client and talk about what's happened in their life since the last visit, and what they have planned for the coming days. Find out if there is anything you can do for them in addition to the regular safeguard visit.

Because this is a short visit, and you'll need to allow for commuting time to and from the client's home, the cost is higher than your normal hourly rate. For example, if you visit for a half-hour, spend ten minutes each way driving to their home, and five minutes emailing your findings to the client's relative, you'll have about an hour invested.

A customary rate for a safeguard visit is the hourly rate, plus 50 percent. For example, if you normally charge $30 an hour, a safeguard visit would be billed at $45.

CHAPTER SEVEN
Resources

Professional organizations for concierges:

- National Concierge Association: **www.ncakey.org**
- National Association of Senior Move Managers: **www.nasmm.org**

Useful books:

- *The Concierge Manual,* by Katherine C. Giovanni
- *How to Say It to Seniors* by David Solie

Useful websites:

- **www.seniorservicebusiness.com** Covers several senior services that do not require specialized training and can be started with a modest amount of money. Services include senior home care, senior relocation, senior home safety consultant and senior transportation. The site also has dozens of helpful articles for anyone considering a senior service business.

- **www.theconciergesociety.com** is the world's largest community of personal concierge business owners with currently over 1100 members. You can join their Facebook group at no charge and learn from the pros.

How to Do a Home Safety Check

Falls at home are a top cause of injuries to older adults. Seniors are also at greater risk of dying in a house fire. Almost all of these injuries are caused by hazards that are easy to overlook, but also easy to fix. After you've done the safety check, be sure to go over the results with your clients to make sure they understand any risks you've found. Offer to work with them to correct any issues

By finding these hazards and taking simple steps to correct them, you can help your senior clients avoid falls and the potential for broken limbs they can cause. Using this basic checklist, you can identify potential hazards in your client's home before they cause an accident. It may take a little time to do a thorough inspection of your client's home, but it could save them thousands of dollars in medical bills – even their life!

- ✓ **Smoke & carbon monoxide (CO) alarms.** Two-thirds of home fire deaths occur in homes without working smoke alarms. A working smoke alarm should be located on every level of a home, outside sleeping areas, and inside bedrooms. A carbon monoxide detector should be installed on every level of a home, and outside sleeping areas. You can now purchase dual alarms that protect against both smoke and carbon monoxide.

Check all smoke and CO alarms once a month to make sure they are operating properly.

✓ **Emergency escape plan.** An escape plan can improve the chances of surviving a fire or similar emergency. Identify at least one way to escape from every room – bedrooms in particular and avoid escape routes that require the use of an escape ladder whenever possible.

✓ **Telephone safety.** Post emergency phone numbers near or on all phones.

Use a telephone with large, lighted numbers if you have vision problems.

Keep telephones at a low height so they can be reached in case of an accident that leaves you unable to stand.

Keep a telephone in each bedroom in case a fire traps you there.

✓ **Walking surfaces.** Tripping over loose carpet or area rugs is a common fall occurrence. Falls account for over half of all emergency room visits for seniors 65-74, and three-quarter of ER visits among seniors over 75 years old.

All home walking surfaces should be flat, slip-resistant and free of electrical cords or any other objects that could be a tripping hazard, especially in case of an emergency or fire.

✓ **Non-skid mats.** Skid-resistant surfaces are a must, especially in potentially wet locations such as bathrooms, entries and kitchens. A non-skid mat or area rug with a non-skid backing can help prevent falls in these high-risk areas.

All area rugs that do not have a non-skid backing should have a separate non-skid mat placed underneath them.

- **Steps and stairways.** All steps and stairways should have flat, even surfaces and be free of objects that could pose a tripping hazard.

  Stair treads should have slip-resistant surfaces, such as low-pile carpeting or slip-resistant strips.

  All stairways should have a light switch at both the top and bottom of the stairs, and a secure, continuous handrail along the full length of the stair, ideally on both sides.

- **Lighting.** Seniors need more light to compensate for vision loss. Check all light fixtures for wattage, and do not use over 60 watt bulbs unless the fixture is labeled for a higher wattage. LED bulbs use much less electricity, so you can have more light at less cost.

  For example, and "old-fashioned" 60 watt light bulb can be replaced with a 15 watt, or less LED bulb, that can provide more light. With bulb lifetimes in the 15-25 year range, a senior may never have to replace a bulb again.

- **Electrical outlets.** All outlets in potentially damp locations, such as a kitchen, bathroom, garage or utility room, and the exterior of the house, should have ground-fault circuit interrupter (GFCI) receptacles installed to protect against electrical shocks.

  Test any existing GFCI outlets, using the built-in test and reset buttons to make sure they are working properly.

- **Electrical cords.** All electrical and other cords should be out of the way of foot traffic paths, as they be a tripping hazard. Never put an electrical cord under a rug or carpet, as it could overheat.

  Make sure the total wattage of all appliances plugged into a standard 16-gauge extension cord do not exceed 1625 watts.

- **Kitchen.** Every kitchen should have a working fire extinguisher and a working ventilation system to remove air pollutants and carbon monoxide from gas appliances.

  A step stool should be close by to allow seniors to reach higher shelves and cabinets safely.

- **Living room and family room.** Chimneys should be inspected by a pro every year and cleaned if necessary.

  Portable space heaters should be a safe distance (usually listed on the heater label) from walls, furniture, or any flammable or combustible material.

  Candles or any smoking material should never be used near combustibles, like curtains or furniture.

- **Bathrooms.** Bathrooms and showers require a non-skid mat, non-skid strips, or a built-in non-skid surface and one or more grab bars.

  Bathroom floor should be slip-resistant or covered with slip-resistant material.

  Keep small electrical appliances, such as hair dryers, shavers and curling irons away from sinks and tubs.

Bathroom electrical receptacles should all be on a GFCI circuit.

✓ **Bedrooms.** Keep ash trays, smoking materials, candles and other potential fire sources away from flammable materials such as curtains, bedding and furniture.

Keep a flashlight within reach of the bed in case of a power outage.

Keep a telephone within reach of a bed in case of emergency.

Never cover, fold or tuck in electrically heated blankets when in use, as it can cause overheating.

✓ **Basements, Garages & Storage Areas.** Set water heaters to no more than 120 degrees F. to help prevent scalding burns.

Older electrical panels with fuses should be checked to make sure the fuses are the correct size. Most residential circuits are on either 15 amp or 20-amp circuits. When possible, an older panel with fuses should be replaced with a modern circuit breaker panel.

All electrical receptacles in garages, workshops and unfinished basements should be protected by GFCI circuits.

All fuel-burning appliances, such as boilers, furnaces, fireplaces, wood stoves and water heaters, and their chimneys, should be professionally inspected yearly.

No containers of flammable or combustible liquids, such as gasoline or kerosene, should be stored inside a house or garage.

Never operate a portable electrical generator inside a home, basement or garage, as they produce high levels of carbon monoxide, which can kill in minutes.

✓ **Home Exterior.** Porches, steps and entries should be well-lit, with a slip-resistant surface. Outside steps require a handrail on at least one side.

Exterior electrical outlets should be GFCI protected and in a weatherproof enclosure.

Check to be sure a senior client can safely use exterior steps. If not, suggest a ramp be installed for safety.

CHAPTER EIGHT

Growing Your Business

Setting Goals

Goal setting is at the top of my "must-do" list for business success. Setting goals helps you think about your future and close the gap between where you are now and where you want to be next year or even further into the future.

The key to goal setting success is writing your goals down on paper. Just the act of writing them down makes them seem real and make them part of your new reality. Get started by writing all the goals for your new business as if you were guaranteed to succeed no matter what.

Think about what you really want, no matter how impossible it may seem to you now. Take some time to dream big! Next, list your goals in order of importance and pick your most important goal. Then ask yourself "What one small step can I take to get me closer to that goal." Then do it today, no matter how small it may seem to you. Just getting started is what counts.

"A goal without a plan is just a wish."

Never forget - every goal, large or small, can be achieved by taking tiny steps every day toward that goal. Breaking your goal into smaller steps can build momentum and reduce the pressure of trying to deal with large goals.

Starting a new business is a large goal, and can seem overwhelming at first glance, but by breaking it down into small daily steps, it becomes much easier and not so overwhelming.

Action Steps:

1. Write down what you really want.
2. Write down how you'll get there.
3. Write down your first step towards your most important goal.

> *"Find something you love to do, and you'll never have to work a day in your life."*
>
> GROUCHO MARX

Setting Realistic Goals

If you don't feel you can reach a goal because it seems overwhelming or you doubt your ability to achieve the goal, it's time to break it down to more manageable "mini-goals."

For example, if your goal of making $100,000 yearly in 2 years with your new business seems too big, break that goal into smaller goals. Set monthly goals, a 6-month goal, and a 1-year goal that are smaller and easier to achieve.

Deadlines

"A goal is a dream with a deadline."

It's important to set deadlines for your goals and the smaller steps to reaching the big goal. For example, say you'll contact 10 potential new customers by October 30th. As you meet your deadlines, you'll build self-confidence and strengthen your belief that your goals are within reach.

Action Step:

Write down deadlines for all your goals - large and small.

"Most people overestimate what they can do in one year, and underestimate what they can do in ten years."

BILL GATES

Most of us are too optimistic when setting goals and making plans. That's why it's not uncommon for things to take longer than expected. If that happens, don't quit or give up! Stick with your goal and realize that you WILL get there, even if it takes a while longer than you thought.

The 80/20 Rule

In working toward your goal, you'll find that 20% of your efforts will bring 80% of your progress towards that goal. This rule may not seem logical, but it has proven to hold true across a wide variety of situations and businesses.

That's why it's important that you find the things that will have the most impact and spend more of your time on them. Here's how to find your personal top 20%:

Make a list of all the things you can think of that could help you achieve your goal. Aim for at least 10 things, 20 is better. Next, ask yourself, "If I could only do one thing on my list, which one will help me the most in reaching my goal?" Now go through the list again and identify the second item that will help you the most. If your list has 10 items, the top 2 gives you your 20%.

Daily Actions

When you work on your goal every day, you'll see progress and help make your goal a reality. By taking small steps every day, you'll feel like your goal is closer and it will empower you to push on.

We all have busy lives, so it's important to set aside enough time each day to work on your goals. Just do what is comfortable at the start, and pledge to stick to it. As you become more at ease with your new daily routine, you can spend more time on it.

"You cannot change your destination overnight, but you can change your direction overnight."

JIM ROHN

If you think you don't have enough time in your day to start a new business, you need to identify the distractions in your life and avoid them or get them under control. Some examples: Turn off your technology alerts! When you need to focus on starting and growing your new business, turn off your email, phone, social media and chat.

Next, stop watching so much television, especially the news. The average person now spends several hours a day watching TV, and you can put that time towards growing a profitable business and a better life. Don't let these distractions control you!

Limiting Beliefs

"Success is nothing more than a few simple disciplines, practiced every day."

Limiting beliefs can hold you back and create a false reality that can keep you from succeeding in your new business. The most common limiting belief when you're starting a new business is "It's too difficult" or "I'm not smart enough."

These limiting beliefs can cause you to put things off or quit at the least sign of failure or difficulty. Having these negative thoughts is normal, but never allow them to prevent you from moving forward.

When you have negative thoughts, give yourself permission to let them go. Replace these negative thoughts and limiting beliefs with more positive and empowering ones. Instead of "I can't do this," use "My new business will allow me to have a life I love."

Visualize Your Success

Imagination is one of the most powerful tools for improving your life and increasing your odds of business success. The more you visualize your goals, the more confident you'll become about your ability to reach those goals.

Take a few minutes every morning to visualize your goals and imagine how you will feel when you reach those goals. This will give you confidence and empower you to continue to take the steps necessary to reach your goals.

Action Steps

1. Focus on positive visualization every day that encourages action.

2. Remove negativity from your life and focus on the positive side. Your glass is half-full, not half-empty!

3. Every day, imagine your business is a huge success, and be confident it will be.

"For things to change, YOU have to change. For things to get better, YOU have to get better. For things to improve, YOU have to improve. When YOU grow, EVERYTHING in your life grows with you."

JIM ROHN

Networking - How to Do It Right

Networking is the most effective way to build your senior transportation business. It cost almost nothing - just your time. It's about building relationships with others with the goal of mutual benefit. It's more than passing out business cards. Networking is a two-way street, not just about trying to get something out of someone.

Networking is also about building trust. People always prefer to buy a product or service from someone they know, like and trust. Think about it. Would you rather let a stranger help your senior parent to the doctor's office or get it done by someone recommended by a friend or business associate?

Yet, if you're shy like me and so many others, just the thought of networking can be intimidating. When networking, remember you are building relationships, not make a sale. Here are a few proven tips to get you started:

1. Be genuine. Don't try to be someone else. If you're not a natural extrovert, that's perfectly okay.

2. Networking is about making friends. If you've ever made friends, you know how to network.

3. No one cares about you. All they care about is themselves. That's why you need to give something to other people you meet, whether they're potential customers or existing clients, without expecting them to do something in return.

4. When you give something to others, it creates an unspoken, often subconscious, need to return the favor. That's why networking works so well.

5. Be visible. Networking is a contact sport and the more people you contact and become visible to, the more you will build your business through networking.

6. When you're talking with someone, listen more than you speak. Give them your full attention and make them feel important by listening to them. When you do that, they will trust, like and respect you.

7. In your conversations with others, practice your ABCs (Always Be Curious). Ask what they do, ask about their family, what they do for fun.

8. Just do it - start a conversation with someone you haven't met yet and don't forget your ABCs.

Networking is an easy way to gain exposure for your new business in the community. Groups such as the Chamber of Commerce, Rotary and Kiwanis, and other business organizations can provide an opportunity to meet, greet, and become better known. Besides groups, spread the word among related businesses, such as senior care managers.

Hiring Employees

Whether you plan to hire new employees now or in the future, it's important to do it right. Because of the complexities of today's labor laws, federal and state regulations and record- keeping involved, you need to know of these requirements before you even place your first help wanted ad.

Hiring the best people for your new senior concierge business will free you to focus on the "big picture" that will help you grow your business, give you a backup person who can take over when you are sick or on vacation and increase your profits as you add new customers.

After you have hired and trained your new employee, you will also gain precious time to keep learning more about your new senior concierge business with workshops and seminars. You'll also gain the time to build your network of prospects which will help your business to grow.

As your business grows, you will gain new customers, but without help, you may have to turn away those new customers because you're already over-extended and over-worked! That's not good. In addition, with good help, you will serve your existing customers better.

When Is It Time to Hire Employees?

1. Do you feel you just can't ever take a day off? Without employees, you can forget vacations or sick days. Just one employee can give you the personal time you need and deserve.

2. Are you turning down new customers? When you have to say "no" to new customers or work longer hours just

to keep up, it's time to get the help that will allow you to expand your business and become more profitable.

3. Are your customers unhappy? When your customers complain about poor service, that's bad for business. It's a sign that you need to add an employee so you can spend more time keeping your customers happy. As I mentioned in an earlier chapter, the customer signs your paycheck.

4. Do you feel overwhelmed by your workload? Do you look forward to your work every day, or do you dread it? When you're stressed or unhappy about your work, it shows, and your customers will sense it. When you love your work, it shows, and a smile on your face sends a huge positive signal to your customers.

5. Do you have a life outside your work? When you neglect your personal life because you're working all the time, guess who suffers? Your family and friends. If this describes you, it may be time to add and employee and get your "real" life back!

6. You want to grow your business, but you never seem to have time to pursue new opportunities or plan your business future. Hiring an employee can give you that vital time to plan for your bigger and better home watch business.

If you found yourself saying "yes" to one or more of these six reasons, read on while we cover the right way to find and hire your first new employee.

How to Find Good Employees

Start with a job description. To attract the right applicants, you need to write a simple job description. Focus on education, experience and "soft skills," such as a "people person" ability to organize and time management.

A G.E.D. or a high school diploma is a reasonable minimum requirement, as senior concierge work requires the ability to read and write at a basic level. Also, I've found new hires with a recent military background to be excellent employees, as the military service has trained them to be punctual, courteous and eager to succeed in the civilian world.

Older folks in their 50s and 60s can also be great hires, especially if your working schedule is flexible. The closer they are to the age of your clients, the greater the ease of communicating with seniors will be. New hires with previous senior care experience can be great hires, and they have proven their ability to do the work with another employer.

Pre - Hiring Setup

Before hiring your first employee, you will need to determine whether you want independent contractors or employees. The main difference between independent contractors and employees is who is in control of the work, according to the I.R.S. and most states.

If someone is responsible for their own work and scheduling, they could be considered an independent contractor. If they depend on you to supply a list of customers, scheduling, and pay, they are considered an employee. There are a lot of "gray areas" here, and laws vary from state to state, so check with your state to find out what their guidelines are.

Background Checks

A pre-employment background check is recommended for all new hires. Better to get any bad news before you hire than after. What information you can check on depends on your state regulations, but almost all states allow a criminal background check and a drug test, the two most important checks for you to consider.

To order a background check, do a web search for "criminal background check in (your state)" Compare prices from at least 3 providers before you order a check. The U.S. Equal Employment Opportunity Commission has strict rules that must be followed if you do a background check. You must notify the applicant in writing that you intend to order a background check.

In addition, the applicant must provide a signed consent to the check. If you are ordering a credit check, the same rules apply, plus you must notify the applicant if you refuse to offer the applicant a job because of information in the credit report.

Drug testing is often included in a complete background check, especially because of the nature of this work. Just imagine for a moment what could happen if a person employed by you was involved in a serious accident while driving a senior client and was found to be driving under the influence of illegal drugs!

Your insurance company would drop your coverage, those injured could sue you and your business could go bankrupt. So just do it! According to the current federal regulations, an applicant can refuse to take a drug test, but if they do, you probably don't want to hire them, anyway.

The U.S. Civil Rights Act makes it illegal to ask about age, race, ethnicity, color, sex, religion, national origin, disabilities, marital status or pregnancy, whether in a background check, an interview or on a written application.

Advertise Your Job

Once you're prepared, it's time to get the word out. Almost all jobs are listed on online job boards. Explore several to see which one might be the best for your employee search.

Here's a list of the larger national job boards:

- Indeed.com
- Careerbuilder.com
- Craigslist.org
- linkedin.com
- Monster.com
- glassdoor.com
- simplyhired.com
- seek.com

Employee Record Keeping and Taxes

First job - insure your new employees. When you hire employees, you must add worker's compensation insurance. This insurance is required in all states and covers injury or illness while on the job.

For an example, if you hired a new employee who injures their back or slips on an icy sidewalk on the job, worker's compensation insurance pays for their medical care and wages while they are unwilling to work.

In most states, worker's compensation insurance is available through private insurance companies. Only four states, Ohio, North Dakota, Washington and Wyoming, have their own state-run insurance plans. If you're in one of the other 46 states, contact your current insurance agent or insurance broker to set up this insurance. Your agent can also add a new employee to your surety bond.

Why Hire a Bookkeeper?

When you add employees, the quantity and complexity of record-keeping can be overwhelming. Don't make the mistake of trying to do everything yourself. Your focus should be on running and growing your senior concierge business.

Few small business owners have the in-depth knowledge of accounts receivable, accounts payable and taxes, and the yearly changes in tax laws and regulations. It's better to hire a professional who has the training and skills to handle this part of your business.

It's also a form of insurance, as missing a bill or a tax filing could affect your business credit rating or result in substantial fees or tax penalties from your state or the I.R.S.

Be sure to hire a bookkeeper that can handle both taxes and payroll so they can handle estimated tax payments, 1099s for independent contractors, Form 940 employment tax forms, W-2 forms and give you a schedule of what is due and when. Unless you enjoy handling these details daily, do yourself a favor and hire a pro!

Never forget … your time is money that can be used towards running your new senior concierge business and taking it to the next level. A good bookkeeper can save you money by ensuring that you don't make costly accounting mistakes, forget to file a form or a tax payment or forget to send reminders when a customer forgets to pay their bill on time.

If you are on a tight budget, you can use one of the bookkeeping software programs covered earlier to handle the more routine tasks, then transfer the data to a pro for the rest. Quicken, for example, is widely used by bookkeepers and accountants, so sharing date with your bookkeeper is almost seamless.

Save on Taxes

Be sure to keep track of all your business-related expenses, as they may be deductible at tax time. Top deductions include:

- ✓ **Vehicle expenses.** At the current 58 cents per mile, this is substantial deduction for most senior concierge businesses. For many, the mileage deduction alone will cover the cost of a new fuel-efficient vehicle in a year or two.

- ✓ **Startup expenses.** The cost of getting your senior concierge business started is usually deductible. Check with a tax guide or tax professional to get specific deductions.

- ✓ **Education expenses.** If you take classes or workshops to maintain or improve your job skills, they may be deductible. Another good reason for attending that convention in Las Vegas next January!

- ✓ **Professional fees.** Fees paid to accountants, tax professionals, lawyers, or other professional consultants are deductible.

- ✓ **Equipment.** Check with a tax pro to see if there are any special "stimulus" deductions available for the purchase of capital equipment such as vehicles and computers.

- ✓ **Interest.** If you use credit to finance business purchases, the interest is deductible.

- ✓ **Advertising.** Any marketing costs, such as a yellow page ad, a magnetic sign for your vehicle or promotional costs, such as sponsoring a little league team or buying equipment for them, is deductible.

An excellent book on the subject is *Deduct It—Lower Your Small Business Taxes,* available at www.nolo.com.

What to Pay Your Employees

To find good employees, you will need to pay competitive wages. If senior care providers in your area are making $16 an hour, you need to match that, or finding the best employees will be difficult.

To get started, go to the help-wanted job boards listed earlier and note hourly wages for similar jobs in your town. Jot down 10 posted rates, then divide by 10 and you've got the magic number you need to match.

While you're checking the job boards, also study the job descriptions. This will help you write an effective ad or post at the job boards. Some job boards, like Indeed, have a template you can use by simple filling in the blanks for important items like job title, start date, pay rate and required background checks.

First, thank you for purchasing and reading this book. I hope it has provided both the resources and the motivation for you to start your own local senior concierge business. Starting your own small business is the ticket to a better life and a prosperous future, and freedom from worries about job security.

If you have a moment, I'd really love a review. Reviews are a huge help to authors, myself included. If you enjoyed this book, please take a minute or two to post a review on Amazon. Just enter the title of this book at Amazon.com, then click on "reviews," then "write a review. Thanks so much for your support!

Wishing you much success in your new business,